SAS® Administration from the Ground Up

Running the SAS®9 Platform in a Metadata Server Environment

Anja Fischer

sas.com/books

The correct bibliographic citation for this manual is as follows: *Fischer, Anja*. 2019. *SAS® Administration from the Ground Up: Running the SAS®9 Platform in a Metadata Server Environment*. Cary, NC: SAS Institute Inc.

SAS® Administration from the Ground Up: Running the SAS®9 Platform in a Metadata Server Environment

Contents

About This Book

What Does This Book Cover?

This book is about the basic principles of SAS 9.4 platform administration. It is a starter guide for new SAS administrators, helping you to turn into a happy, calm and confident SAS admin. The book provides you with a light entrance into the world of SAS administration, without wading through the documentation. This book does not cover SAS Viya administration.

Is This Book for You?

If you are new to the SAS 9.4 admin job or are an advanced admin who wants to make sure you know all the admin basics and admin tricks, this book is for you.

What Should You Know about the Best Practices?

This book provides recommendations and best practices around the most important SAS 9.4 platform administration topics a SAS Platform administrator should be familiar with.

Additional Resources

Please find an appendix full of handy links and references on the author's page at http://support.sas.com/fischer.

We Want to Hear from You

Do you have questions about a SAS Press book that you are reading? Contact us at saspress@sas.com.

SAS Press books are written *by* SAS Users *for* SAS Users. Please visit sas.com/books to sign up to request information on how to become a SAS Press author.

We welcome your participation in the development of new books and your feedback on SAS Press books that you are using. Please visit sas.com/books to sign up to review a book

Learn about new books and exclusive discounts. Sign up for our new books mailing list today at https://support.sas.com/en/books/subscribe-books.html.

Learn more about this author by visiting her author page at http://support.sas.com/fischer. There you can download free book excerpts, access the appendix, read the latest reviews, get updates, and more.

Acknowledgments

So many people contributed to this – thank you all!

My wonderful fur-kids: Thank you for putting up with me and for not being mad at me for some non-taken-walks. I'm not upset anymore about y'all digging a Grand Canyon in our backyard while my head was in the book.

Lauree Shepard, my editor: Thank you for your great support and help throughout this book adventure and for patiently keeping up with my "it-has-to-be-fun-and-special-and-here-is-another-idea-and-please-more-color" moments.

Reviewers: Michelle and Paul Homes, David Stern, Juan Sanchez, Margaret Crevar, Mark Schneider, Scott McCauley. Thank you so much for all your great input. Special thanks to Michelle, Paul and David for sharing their awesome security knowledge with me.

Shelley Sessoms: Thank you so much for encouraging me to write this book and for supporting me.

My managers and director, T Winand, Rick McElroy and Christina Harris: Thank you for letting me write the book and for supporting me.

Beate: Your "whenever-we-talk-you-say-its-only-three-more-chapters" talks challenged me to write faster. We did it!

Twanda and Krystal: I appreciate your "butt kicks" in my "am-so-done" moments after all night writing! It was so worth it!

Kevin: We make the best admin team! There is no-one I'd rather fight the admin beast with, my dear admin pal!

Mom and Dad: Please don't sell my book to all your friends in your "WE ARE SOOOOO PROUD" spirit. I doubt we can interest them in SAS administration!

This book is dedicated to Jasper – the best pal ever – and to all the SAS admins in this world.

Yours,

Anja

Sr Systems Engineer and passionate SAS admin
SAS Institute

Chapter 1: Congratulations, You're the SAS Administrator! Now What??

Why a starter-admin book?

SAS administration can be complex, maybe even frustrating at times. It might drive you crazy, but once you know the drill and once you have the right head start, you will see that it can, in fact, be fun (this is not sarcastic, I am serious).

Increasingly, I came to realize that many SAS administrators do not have the luxury of getting training. Often, they, are on their own and must figure things out by themselves. Talking to many advanced SAS admins throughout the years, they found that the most challenging part of becoming an admin was actually knowing how, and where, to get started.

An admin needs to understand the entire SAS environment. If the software that is licensed is not set up and not used properly, it pretty much defeats the purpose.

Once you have finished this book, you will be ready to go!

What the book will and won't cover:

Some specific topics this book covers (and does not cover) include:

- SAS 9.4 administration in a single- or multi-machine metadata server environment.
- SAS SAS Viya administration is not covered. You can read up on SAS Viya administration here:
  SAS Viya 3.4 Administration: Orientation
  https://go.documentation.sas.com/?cdcId=calcdc&cdcVersion=3.4&docsetId=calchkcfg&docsetTarget=n00004saschecklist0000config.htm&locale=en
- Other SAS 9 versions might be called out in between, but this book is about SAS 9.4.
- This book applies to Windows, Linux and UNIX platforms. Mainframe administration will not be covered.

- Product additions (SAS Grid, SAS Visual Analytics, etc.) and solutions (such as SAS Marketing Automation for example) are not part of this book. Even though additional products and solutions are not covered, here comes the kicker: even though you might have SAS solutions or, SAS Grid, or maybe SAS Visual Analytics, you still must know how to administer the underlying SAS system. So, no matter what, you are not getting around learning the basics of SAS administration.

Finally, there are a lot of useful links included in this book – not so useful if you have the print version! So all these links can be found in a pdf on my author page to save on typing!

And off we go ... Happy reading!

Chapter 2: Let the Admin Fun Begin: SAS 9.4 Architecture

Introduction

The starting point for SAS administration is the architecture: what are the components of a *SAS deployment*, how does it look? With a good understanding of the SAS architecture, you'll be able to tackle the responsibilities and tasks that come with SAS administration. Understanding the architecture means you know where to look if you need to make any changes, troubleshoot, and the like.

The best way to explain the SAS 9.4 environment architecture is an analogy to the architecture of a house. Envision the following:

You buy a piece of land (infrastructure/hardware). You want to build a new house (software) on your land. How do you build your house (install your software)? You need an architect (an admin). Sometimes there is one architect, sometimes there are more than one (one admin vs many admins). Once you decide on the shape, storage, levels, house color etc. first thing the home builders do is lay down a foundation (SAS metadata server). On top of that, the walls are built for either a one-story or multiple-story house (distributed or non-distributed SAS environment).

Once the house is built and is move-in ready, you have bedrooms, guest room, kid's room, office, kitchen, bathroom, etc., each of which has a different purpose (a different "task"). The different floors, the different rooms, are your SAS servers, each of which fulfills different tasks, different needs - a different purpose.

Last but not least, think about the different objects in these rooms: toys, towels, beds, plates, glasses, toothbrushes etc. All these objects can be compared with data sources: SAS data sets, DBMS, Hadoop etc. Knowing what is in each room helps find what you are looking for. Same with SAS architecture: if you know and understand the architecture, you know where to look.

Now, your house is completed, and you have moved in. You're done. Right?

Very wrong. After you move in to this great new home, you must maintain it to keep it great, clean and beautiful. Think about it: You must wash the windows, change the air filters, check the air conditioner at least twice a year, do dishes, vacuum, etc.– some of the tasks more frequently than others. Same concept with SAS: once it is installed, you must maintain it to keep it clean, healthy and good looking. So, lets apply the house analogy to SAS.

Let's start with the different install flavors (single house versus townhouse, single story versus multiple stories). SAS can be installed either as a SAS Foundation install or as a metadata managed install.

> **Note:** In this book, we will focus on metadata managed deployments only!

SAS Foundation is your basic install, think Base SAS. A metadata managed install is the SAS 9 Intelligence Platform, with much more than Base SAS. You might have SAS Visual Analytics, Grid, SAS solutions, SAS Add-In for Microsoft Office, etc. With SAS Foundation, your users work on their personal machines, or use Remote Desktop or Citrix. A SAS Foundation install does not involve a centrally metadata managed system. In a metadata managed install, your users work on the dedicated SAS server.

The two different SAS deployments can be installed on physical or virtual machines.

> **Note**: For every SAS solution, every Grid install, SAS Visual Analytics (and more), the SAS Platform administration applies. Even though Grid, VA and SAS solutions have additional, product-specific administration tasks: EVERY PRODUCT IS BASED ON SAS 9.4 PLATFORM ADMINISTRATION!

Let's take a peek at the SAS Configuration. We will only cover it briefly, to give you some very basics.

SAS Configuration Directories

After SAS is installed, you'll find two different SAS directories. One called **SASHOME** and another one, called **Lev1** (aka configuration directory) for the metadata managed, site-specific configuration for your SAS 9 platform services.

New admins are often taken by surprise that SAS has two directories, and don't quite know what to do with them. I totally get it. So, let's see whether we can shed some light on this "dual" directory situation.

SASHome

SASHOME includes subfolders for all your SAS desktop clients and SAS web clients. This directory (aka SAS root folder) is located per default at:

- C:\Program Files\SASHome on Windows, and
- /usr/local/SASHome on Linux/Unix.

Depending on the way SAS is installed, !SASHOME can be at another location

On Windows, for example, SASHOME might look like:

Figure 2.1: SASHOME directory

Note: Depending on the products you have licensed, you might have different folders.

Aside from executables and configuration files in each respective client folder, you find some other cool things, such as examples, SAS programs and data that is specific to that client.

Take SAS Enterprise Guide for example. Look at

SASHome\SASEnterpriseGuide\7.1\Sample and you'll find code examples, data sets, and Enterprise Guide example projects.

If users run tests and do not want to touch production, or new users must come up to speed with SAS Enterprise Guide, these are some examples of situations where this test data might come in handy.

Another example is the *SASFoundation* folder, in which you can find example data sets, programs, catalogs and views: **\SASHome\SASFoundation\9.4\core\sample**

> **Note:** The SASFoundation folder also stores your setinit information:
> **!SASHome\SASFoundation\9.4\core\sasinst**
>
> The setinit is your license file. This file includes the products your company has licensed and the date when the license expires.

Lev1/Levn

Lev1/Levn is the metadata managed, site-specific configuration for your SAS 9 platform services. The default path for the configuration directory is **\SAS-config-dir\Lev1** where "SAS-config-dir" is the path that you chose during the deployment.

Just as with SASHOME, the configuration directory **\SAS-config_dir\Lev1** includes configuration files, scripts, etc. An example for a site-specific configuration directory is shown in Figure 2.2.

Figure 2.2: Lev1 Directory

> **Note:** Depending on the products you have licensed, the directory structure might look differently.
>
> **Note:** In some deployments you might find a *Lev2* and/or *Lev3*. In such cases it simply means that one might have set up a dev, test, and prod environment, or, runs different SAS 9 versions in parallel.

The following lists the content of the Levn subdirectory.

Contents of the Levn Subdirectory
(Resource: SAS® 9.4 Intelligence Platform: Administration / System Administration, available at:
https://go.documentation.sas.com/?cdcId=bicdc&cdcVersion=9.4&docsetId=bisag&docsetTarget=p1oa9ysgpowj4vn19o67gc7xrrr0.htm&locale=en)

Subdirectory or File	Description
AppData	Contains indexes and the repository configuration file for the SAS Content Server, and data that is installed for the use of specific applications (for example, SAS BI Dashboard).
Backup/Vault	Is the default location for backups that are created by the Deployment Backup and Recovery Tool.
ConnectSpawner	Contains the management script, configuration files, and logs for the SAS/CONNECT spawner.
Data	Can be used to store user data.
DeploymentTesterServer	Contains files that are used by the Deployment Tester plug-in to SAS Management Console.
Documents	Contains Instructions.html, which contains post-installation configuration instructions; DeploymentSummary.html; ConfigurationErrors.html; and other application-specific documents .Tip: The **instructions.html** file includes all information about how SAS was installed, errors or warnings that might have occurred during the install, links, ports and other helpful information. You can look at that file to find out about configuration paths, log file locations, links etc. It can be helpful to familiarize yourself with your SAS install. Aside from the instructions.html file, there are other helpful information available. The next table lists some of them as examples.

Subdirectory or File	Description
Logs	Can be used as a common directory for server and spawner logs, if you selected this option during a custom installation. By default, each server has its own separate log directory.
Logs/Configure	Contains logs that are created by the SAS Deployment Wizard.
ObjectSpawner	Contains a management script, configuration files, and logs for the object spawner.
SASApp	Contains management scripts, configuration files, and logs for SAS Application Server components
SASMeta	Contains management scripts, configuration files, metadata repositories, logs, and other files and directories for the SAS Metadata Server. .
ShareServer	Contains the management script, configuration information, and log files for the SAS/SHARE server.
Utilities	Contains XML files that are used as input to the SAS Deployment Wizard and utilities that are associated with this configuration instance.
Web	See Contents of the Web Subdirectory.
WebInfrastructurePlatformDataServer	Contains the management script, configuration information, and log files for the SAS Web Infrastructure Platform Data Server.
generate_boot_scripts.sh	Is a script that is used to regenerate the sas.servers script on UNIX.
metadataConfig.xml	Provides information for application server components to use when they connect to a clustered metadata server.
sas.servers	Is a management script that is used on UNIX to start, stop, or restart all servers on the machine in the correct order, or to display the status of all servers on the machine.
sasv9_meta.cfg	Specifies metadata server connection information for the SAS OLAP Server and SAS/SHARE server.

SAS Tiers: The three plus one SAS Tiers in a metadata-managed environment

The SAS **Lev***n* configuration is only one part of the SAS Platform. It is also important to know that your environment is an n-tier architecture, which means that all components that make up your SAS environment, can be distributed over multiple computer resources. Each tier component, each tier part, performs only the work it is responsible for.

Depending on the number of servers you have available, the SAS tiers can be installed across multiple machines or on a single machine. Going back to our analogy at the beginning: each room fulfills a different purpose, "stores" different objects, serves different members of a family. All of the rooms together make your house (SAS deployment). Now, what are these tiers?

Getting to grips with the SAS tiers truly is a fundamental requirement for a good SAS administrator. In SAS 9, we have three tiers, plus one. Plus one, because the fourth tier is not a SAS tier, but is an important element. Let's investigate each tier a bit further.

SAS Servers Tier aka Compute Tier

Simply put: SAS servers perform SAS processing on your data. They are SAS Server processes running on one or more physical or virtual server machines.

Important – and often misunderstood: The tiers are not actual physical machines, but processes, where each process (SAS server) has its own tasks. One function is providing your users with the data they are requesting, or, running a Stored Process, or creating a report. And that's really all there is to it: the tier these SAS processes (SAS servers) are running on is referred to as Server Tier or Compute Tier.

Next, we have the web tier, called the middle tier.

Middle Tier aka Web Tier

The middle tier – also called the web tier – coordinates the web traffic. It enables access to data and functionality using web clients, a browser. Think SAS Studio (users using a web browser), SAS Environment Manager (web client) or any other web-based SAS APIs. We will revisit the middle tier in a little bit.

Client Tier

The client tier runs your desktop clients and web browsers. Examples for SAS clients are SAS Enterprise Guide, SAS Add-In for Microsoft Office, SAS Enterprise Miner, and so on.

Data Tier (Data Sources) – The "Plus One" Tier

The data tier is where the data sources are stored. It is different from the SAS tiers we just described because even though it is important to SAS, it does not come from SAS. It is not used for SAS to run but for users to consume using SAS.

A data tier can be any machine that stores data that you want to access from within SAS.

Data sources can be SAS data sets, OLAP cubes, web content, DBMS data (SAS can access databases such as Oracle as one example out of many), and more. We will talk more about data in Chapter 5, Metadata Library Administration.

Table 2.1 depicts the three plus one tiers. Even though the tiers are pictured in four different boxes, the boxes do not represent physical machines. It simply pictures the different layers a

SAS metadata deployment consists of, whether it is installed on one machine or multiple machines.

Table 2.1: Architecture of the SAS Intelligence Platform

Data Tier	SAS Server Tier	Middle Tier	SAS Client Tier
SAS Data Sets OLAP Cubes SAS Scalable Performance Data Server (SPDS) SAS Web Infrastructure Platform Data Server Third-Party Data Sources (such as Oracle, Teradata, etc.) Hadoop Enterprise Resource Planning (ERP) Systems	SAS Metadata Server SAS Workspace Server SAS Pooled Workspace Server SAS OLAP Server SAS Stored Process Server *These servers are running SAS processes for distributed clients*	SAS Web Server --- SAS Web Application Server SAS Web Infrastructure Platform **Task:** providing services and applications for SAS web applications. It includes: SAS Content Server to store digital content (such as reports) and other infrastructure applications and service *(such as SAS Deployment Backup and Recovery tool, and more)* Web Clients: (run in an instance of the SAS Web Application Server). The SAS web clients are: SAS Web Report Studio SAS Information Delivery Portal SAS BI Portlets SAS BI Dashboard SAS Help Viewer for the Web Other SAS Web Applications and Solutions --- SAS Environment Manager (server process that includes a web application server, providing a web-based administrative interface)	Desktop Clients: SAS Add-In for Microsoft Office SAS Data Integration Studio SAS Enterprise Miner SAS Forecast Studio SAS Enterprise Guide SAS Information Map Studio SAS Management Console SAS Model Manager SAS OLAP Cube Studio SAS Workflow Studio JMP Other SAS analytics products and solution --- Web Browser to surface web Applications --- Mobile Devices, if applicable, to view certain type of reports

Figure 2.3 shows this from a very simplified layer perspective.

Figure 2.3: A layered view of SAS platform architecture.

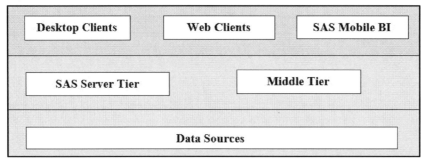

To take a closer look at these tiers, take a look at the Architecture Overview section in *SAS® 9.4 Intelligence Platform: Administration / SAS Intelligence Platform: Overview*, available at: .https://go.documentation.sas.com/?cdcId=bicdc&cdcVersion=9.4&docsetId=biov&docsetTarget=titlepage.htm&locale=en

SAS Server Tier

Let's come back and talk a bit more about the SAS Server tier. I would like to spend some time discussing its components because as a SAS administrator, this is super important!

To refresh your memory, SAS servers are SAS Server processes running on one or more physical or virtual server machines. The SAS server tier is nothing but a bucket of SAS processes that are based on "sas.exe". Every "sas.exe" has a different role or functionality, such as:

- metadata server (in-memory)
- workspace server (interactive sessions)
- stored process and pooled workspace server (trusted sessions)
- if you have SAS Visual Analytics for example, the SAS LASR Analytic Servers (in-memory for SAS Visual Analytics). We will not address SAS Visual Analytics; this is simply meant as an example.

Let's discuss each of these in turn.

Metadata Server

The metadata server is the heart of your environment, the foundation. If it's not working, SAS is not working. Going back to the house-building analogy: if the foundation is weak or breaks, the house will crumble.

The metadata server is an in-memory server. It keeps your environment running and stores all your assets: metadata about where to find your assets, where assets can be data, users and groups, etc. It is a centralized resource for storing, managing, and also providing metadata for all your SAS applications, for all your users.

In-memory: when your users request data, a copy of the physical data is stored into memory. From there on, your users are going "against" memory. This speeds up the process so that the access time is quicker. Memory is flushed when you pause and resume, or, stop and restart the metadata server.

When speaking about metadata assets, we are referring to libraries, users, groups, SAS folders – everything you create using SAS Management Console or SAS® 9.4 Open Metadata

Interface (metadata server programming language). SAS applications also create and manage metadata.

To learn more about the SAS 9.4 Open Metadata Interface, take a look at https://go.documentation.sas.com/api/docsets/omaref/9.4/content/omaref.pdf

These assets are stored in a *metadata repository*. A repository is like a box in which you save all your belongings. Your main repository is *Foundation*. You can also create custom and project repositories. When SAS is installed, only one repository is created, which is the Foundation one.

A custom repository can be used – as one example – in cases where you might have very sensitive data that should only be available to a certain group of users. The custom repository and its contents could be created in a directory where only these users have access to.

Project repositories are used for Change Management and are available for SAS Data Integration Studio only. Users can check out and lock metadata so that metadata can be modified and tested, to be checked back in afterward, which then unlocks the metadata.

In this book, we will focus on the Foundation repository. To learn more about custom and project repositories, check out About Repositories at https://go.documentation.sas.com/?cdcId=bicdc&cdcVersion=9.4&docsetId=bisag&docsetTarget=p1b7gxgkbu04zbn1dhnh3pb8c6zs.htm&locale=en

When you log on to SAS Management Console, *Foundation* is chosen per default as shown in Figure 2.4.

Figure 2.4: SAS Management Console

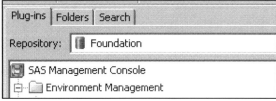

> **Note:** The path defaults to
> `SAS-conf-dir/Lev1/SASMeta/MetadataServer/MetadataRepositories/`.
> Do not rename or delete the metadata server repository path and never move, delete, or
> modify data sets in the MetadataRepositories and rposmgr directories.

You can remove metadata objects via SAS Management Console or by using metadata
programming features using the SAS® 9.4 Open Metadata Interface. Before you delete or
remove any metadata objects, I recommend the following information from the
sasCommunity.org Planet: "*Where is my stuff? Documenting what is stored in SAS Metadata*"
available at: http://www.sascommunity.org/planet/blog/category/metadata/.
Note: if you are using the printed book version, I realize that having to type a link into a web
browser is a bit laborious, but this is one of the articles that are really helpful, and hard to find
if you don't dig deep. Typing it is worth it.

Metadata server and system access

You can use the metadata server's authorization model to control access to your SAS assets
(aka metadata objects). SAS security does not include protection of configuration files or any
non-SAS-related content. In the Appendix of the book, you will find an overview of the
operating system protections for Windows and Unix/Linux. Chapter 6, SAS 9.4 Metadata
Security will cover metadata server authorization.

How about a clustered metadata server? Let's talk high availability!

You have the option to set up the SAS Metadata Server as a clustered configuration. A
metadata server cluster provides redundancy and high availability, which helps you make
sure your environment will continue to operate should one metadata server go down.

You can implement metadata server clustering at any time. It does not have to be set up
during the initial install.

A common question is if the SAS clients know when one cluster node goes down and another
one picks up. There is no configuration for your SAS clients necessary. SAS clients, such as
SAS Management Console, keep a list of the metadata server cluster nodes, which is updated
each time a client connects to the cluster.

Where changes are required is for the SAS Application Server tier. Application servers such
as the Object Spawner, workspace server, stored process server, etc. don't understand that
there is a cluster all of a sudden. Application servers use a configuration file – called
metadataConfig.xml – which tells them about the metadata server. So as long as you don't
make changes to this file, the SAS application servers still assume that there is only one
metadata server. The SAS middle tier applications keep a list that is automatically updated
when the Web Infrastructure Platform web application starts. This is all described in the
information for metadata server clustering, which you will find in the resource references in
the Appendix of this chapter.

In addition to the official SAS documentation about metadata server clustering, you will find
some other great resources such as papers and blogs.

How do clients interact with the metadata server?

When users start a SAS client, such as SAS Enterprise Guide, a connection profile is used to connect to the metadata server. I will talk about Connection Profiles a little later in this chapter.

Metadata Server logging

The default location for the Metadata Server log file is:

```
SAS-config-dir\\Lev1\SASMeta\MetadataServer\Logs
```

SAS 9.4 uses a standard logging facility to perform logging for the metadata server and all other SAS servers. Generally, the default logging information are sufficient, as it provides you with information, warnings and errors. SAS Technical Support might ask you to increase the logging level if more precise information is needed for troubleshooting. You can certainly modify the logging levels at any time. Just keep in mind that increasing the information the metadata server writes to the log, the metadata server log file size will grow. Maintaining log files will be discussed further in the housekeeping chapter.

Note: If the reason for considering enabling additional logging is because you want more information for auditing and monitoring, logging will not fulfill your needs. In Chapter 3, SAS Administration Tools, we will talk about SAS Environment Manager, which provides you with some great options for monitoring or auditing.

Important: If you look at the individual log folders for your SAS servers, you will notice that the workspace server does not have any log files. A workspace server log is written for each individual user. Let your users work for a day with a workspace server log enabled and you'll end up with an abundance of log files. Workspace server logs are usually only enabled when SAS Technical Support needs information for further troubleshooting. Enabling workspace server logging just out of curiosity can affect the performance.

About the Workspace Server, Stored Process Server and all other SAS Servers

These servers are called SAS Application Servers. The SAS Application Servers are a set of metadata objects using application server specific configuration files that are automatically created when SAS is installed. You can look at the SAS Application Server definitions in SAS Management Console, Server Manager. The SAS Application Server Context is called SASApp by default.

Most SAS Application Servers are structured with a Logical Server component and a Server component. Figure 2.5 is an example for the Stored Process Server.

Figure 2.5: Stored Process Server Structure

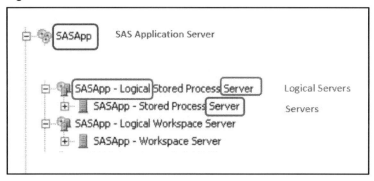

The SAS Application Servers are simply SAS processes, fulfilling all different types of user requests. The workspace server is used for general client user interactions. The stored process server is used for stored processes, and so on.

> **Note:** You must not rename the name *SASApp*. Configuration files use this name reference and its configuration settings for SAS client interactions. Renaming SASApp could result in your users not being able to run jobs within SAS clients.

Underneath the *SASApp*, you can see the various dependent SAS Application Server objects, and the way they are structured. Almost all server components consist of a *Logical Server* component and a *Server* component.

Logical Servers and Servers

SAS servers, such as the workspace server or stored process server for example, can be grouped into logical objects. That means, you can have multiple servers grouped together under one logical application server.

Let's stick with the SAS workspace server for a moment. An example for server definitions under a **Logical Server** definition is:

But it could also look like

As you can see in this example, a *Logical Server* can have one Workspace Server definition or multiple. In this case, I created two additional workspace servers based on the department I work in, called Customer Success. In this department, we have a group of Systems Engineers and Customer Success Managers. We separate the workspace servers for both groups for purposes such as:

- You want a certain group of users to run their jobs in a specific application server. Every time a user (such as a Systems Engineer) runs a job, the job is executed by a specific workspace server (*Systems Engineers Workspace Server*).

- You can also use it if you want to assign certain content. We could assign specific SAS libraries to each individual group, as in our case, libraries for Systems Engineers and libraries for Customer Success Managers.

Additional logical servers are created using the SAS Deployment Wizard.

Another example for a scenario in which the creation of additional servers might make sense is in a dev, test and prod environment.

Creating dev, test, prod environments (additional SAS 9.4 instances) is a big topic in itself, and the example for creating additional servers for a dev, test, prod environment is just one example. Another way to set up multiple SAS 9.4 instances is with the SAS Migration Utility. The Appendix of this chapter will provide you with the resource reference, talking about how to copy existing deployments to create additional SAS 9 instance using the SAS Migration Utility.

There are many great discussions about this topic on the SAS Administration and Deployment Community. One of which I would like to highlight is *Running two SAS Environments on the same Linux machine.*

The question was if there is a best practice for deploying SAS 9.4 on the same machine to create additional separate environments. In this case, the user was looking to create a second SAS 9.4 instance on the same machine. Paul Homes, an expert and owner of the SAS partner metacoda, provided some great information that I would like to share with you. The question was for Linux, but the concept can be applied to other operating systems flavors as well. I would like you to focus on the pros and cons described. Paul's answer to the question:

You can definitely run 2 environments on the same machine (given the machine is suitably sized in terms of memory, CPU, storage, etc.). Use the SAS Deployment Manager to do an install and deployment of Lev1 and then run it again to do another deployment of Lev2. You can choose different Lev numbers as long as they are different for each environment on the same machine. By choosing a different Lev number all of the default port numbers will be automatically chosen to avoid conflict.

Of course, there is also the option to have multiple virtual machines on the same physical machine.

If you are not installing new 'empty' environments then the SAS Migration Utility can be used to create a package based on an existing SAS environment so you can use it during the deployment of a new environment. Alternatively, you can use the export/import tools to migrate metadata and content using SAS package files post-install.

A benefit of having both environments on the one machine is one less machine to procure and manage. A downside is that the machine will need to be bigger to support both environments. Being less isolated can also make it harder to do changes to one environment without potentially impacting the other environment. (...) Imagine a DEV and PROD on the same machine. You wouldn't be able to test opsys and SAS patches on DEV prior to their application to PROD. You wouldn't be able to reboot the DEV machine without rebooting the (same) PROD machine.

As to whether the pros outweight the cons or vice-versa depends on how you plan to use the environments. I would definitely recommend consulting SAS Professional Services or a local SAS Partner if you want some help with planning.

I went a bit of track there, let's get back to our SAS Application Servers ...

SAS Application Servers are accessed either by desktop clients or, by web applications that run in the middle tier. Logical Servers are "holding" the Servers that you have per default, plus, any custom servers should you decide to add them. The workspace server is just an example. It is the same concept for other SAS Application Servers as well.

Logical Servers contain one – and one only – application server definition, such as the workspace server. The object name SASApp – Workspace Server or SASApp – Stored Process Server etc., hold the information for the server that executes SAS code. If you look at the properties for the SASApp – Workspace Server for example, you'll see the following:

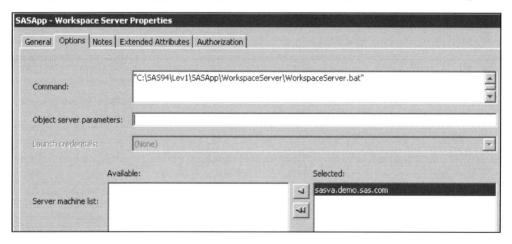

The file WorkspaceServer.bat includes the information needed to start the workspace server and the selected server machine is the machine where the server runs on. Customers create additional servers to separate group access, as one example.

The hardcopy readers amongst us are probably getting close to hit me with my admin book, because I would like – once more – highlight a paper that goes with the SAS workspace server and might come in handy should you ever experience any delays with the SAS workspace server initialization. But remember all these links can be found on my author page in a handy pdf. The paper is called: Tracking Down the Culprit of a SAS® Workspace Server Initialization Delay, available at https://www.sas.com/content/dam/SAS/support/en/sas-global-forum-proceedings/2018/2003-2018.pdf.

SAS Connection Profiles

While we are talking about the SAS servers and services, users, and client products such as SAS Enterprise Guide, I believe that SAS connection profiles are worth mentioning.

Logging In

When users log on to a client, or an admin logs on an admin tool – whether it is a desktop or web client – a connection profile is used. Then, users or admins connect to the metadata server. In order for the web or desktop clients to "find" the metadata server, we need the metadata server "address," aka connection profile. The connection profile simply stores user credentials, ports, and server names. You can find the profiles in the following location for SAS Data Integration Studio, SAS Information Map Studio, SAS Management Console and SAS OLAP Cube Studio:

- Windows Vista or later: C:\Users\user-name\AppData\Roaming\SAS\MetadataServerProfiles
- UNIX: /user-home/SASAppData/MetadataServerProfiles.

The client profiles have the extension **swa**. Here is a snippet of a client profile:

port=8561

userid=sasdemo

Name=SASDemo

password={sas002}1D57933958C580064BD3DCA81A33DFB2

host=machine_name

In this profile, the user name and password are stored, which means the user will not be prompted. The users have the option to check a box during login that saves the user ID and password in their profile.

> **Tip:** If you would like to avoid that users have the option to check this check box, you can do the following:
> On your metadata server machine, go to
> `sas_config_dir\Lev1\SASMeta\MetadataServer` and open the file
> `omaconfig.xml`.
>
> Change the value for SASEC_LOCAL_PW_SAVE from 1 to 0, where 1 is YES and 0 is NO.
>
> Save your changes and close the file.
>
> Restart your metadata server for the changes to take effect. Please keep in mind that the restart of the metadata server will throw out all your users, meaning, their work will be interrupted. For that reason, you might want to choose a time where there is the least user traffic.
>
> This will disable the check box to save user ID and password from the profile.

Quick excursion to SAS encryption

Looking at the client's .swa file, you might notice the password:

`password={sas002}1D57933958C580064BD3DCA81A33DFB2.`

SAS encrypts password at rest and in transit. There are several encryption mechanisms available in SAS. Here, you see sas002, which is the default SAS encryption called *SASProprietary*, which is a fixed coding algorithm with medium security.

OK, that was the SAS Application Servers. Next, I would like to take a moment and look at the SAS Object Spawner.

Object Spawner

Another important SAS component that we must talk about when talking about SAS application servers is the Object Spawner. An object spawner runs on each machine where you want to run a workspace server, pooled workspace server or stored process server.

The Object Spawner's task is it to launch a workspace server, pooled workspace server or stored process server, whenever one is requested. If a user accesses a table in SAS Enterprise Guide to work with it, the workspace server is used to execute the user's job, right? Not quite. The component that actually starts a workspace server session is the Object Spawner.

Before the Object Spawner starts any of these application servers, it establishes a communication with the metadata server to check whether the requesting user has a valid user ID.

To be able to have a communication between the Object Spawner and the metadata server, the object spawner uses a configuration file that includes the information needed to access the metadata server. The configuration file is called **metadataConfig.xml** and is located at **SAS-config-dir\Lev1\ObjectSpawner**.

It includes the metadata server machine, the metadata server port and other information. Think of it as if you are giving someone your address to find you.

The SAS documentation uses the following figure to show how the spawner obtains metadata:

❶ The object spawner accesses the metadataConfig.xml

The object spawner connects to the SAS Metadata Server for configuration information.

It is like me asking my German pal where I can get the best Bratwurst. She gives me the name of a store and I take that information to get to the store. (quite the example, isn't).

Authentication and starting SAS Servers

Example for Workspace server:

Before the Object spawner starts a workspace server, the metadata server provides credential information and details about how to start the server. In a default scenario, the object spawner uses host authentication, which means the workspace server is started under the users' credentials.

After the client – such as SAS Enterprise Guide – is exited, the workspace server session is closed. You can use token-authentication instead of host authentication. Token authentication uses a shared user and generates a single-use identity token.

Let's take a look at it:

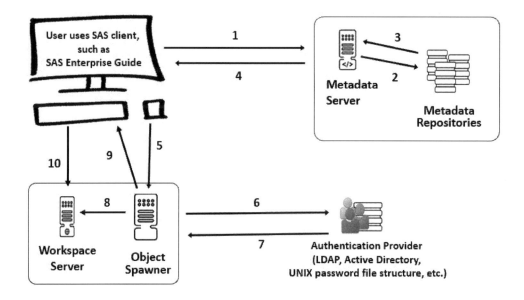

The steps in detail:

1. Using the already established connection to the metadata server, the SAS client, here the user is using SAS Enterprise Guide, requests access to a workspace serve (1)

2. In step 2, the metadata server searches the metadata (metadata repositories) for the workspace server in question.

3. The metadata server then gets the machine name hosting the workspace server, the Object Spawners's port and an authentication domain that is associated with the workspace serve (we will address authentication domains in the security chapter).

4. This connection information is returned to SAS Enterprise Guide.

5. SAS Enterprise Guide uses the connection information to make the request for a workspace server. If the authentication domain for the server matches that of the initial inbound login, SAS Enterprise Guide passes along the credentials as well.

6. The authentication domain comes into play for the credentials that are being used. If the user ID is not associated with the default authentication domain (called DefaultAuth), SAS Enterprise Guide searches its in-memory list of credentials to find the user's credentials with the appropriate authentication domain. If no user credential is found, SAS Enterprise Guide queries the metadata server for credentials for this user for that particular authentication domain (outbound login). If none is found, the user will be prompted for credentials.

7. The object spawner sends the user's credentials to its authentication provider. The default authentication provider is the host. As shown in the graph above, different authentication providers can be used.

8. The authentication provider verifies that the credentials are valid.

9.   The object spawner launches the workspace server. It uses the launch command that was retrieved from the metadata at start-up. The workspace server runs under the credentials provided by SAS Enterprise Guide, that have been authenticated by the host.

10. The object spawner provides SAS Enterprise Guide with a TCP connection to the workspace server session.

SAS Enterprise Guide communicates directly with the workspace server.

Now, the user submits requests with SAS Enterprise Guide for processing. Results are returned to SAS Enterprise Guide. Easy as that: Code submitted, results returned

My Bratwurst example sounded simpler.

There are great troubleshooting tips available for SAS servers. Because I am afraid to add yet another note apologizing to the hardcopy readers for my long web addresses, I am going to spoof this link situation up a notch and simply say: Google for "SAS 9.4 Troubleshooting the SAS Server Tier" and you will find helpful troubleshooting tips for SAS servers.

In case you run into any problems/errors/warnings with the SAS object spawner, here are the log locations:

SAS Object Spawner log file locations:

SAS object spawner log files are located here:

> Windows:
> **configuration-directory\ObjectSpawner\logs**
> UNIX:
>
> **configuration-directory/ObjectSpawner/logs**

And on to the next tier ...

Middle Tier

The middle tier, or web tier, enables access with a web browser using web clients. It is pretty straight forward. Examples for web clients are SAS Studio or SAS Environment Manager.

> **Tip:** If you don't know the links to access these clients, you can look at the `instructions.html` file, which is located per default in your configuration directory: `\config_dir\Lev1\Documents`

The middle tier includes the following components:

- SAS Web Application Server and SAS Web Server (http server)
- Cache Locator

- JMS Broker
- SAS Environment Manager

SAS Web Application Server and SAS Web Server (http server)

SAS 9.4 has its own web server and web application server. This is good news because it doesn't require the installation of any third-party web app products, such as IBM WebSphere or JBoss Application Server. During the SAS install, the middle tier is installed and configured for you.

The SAS Web Application Server is based on a commercially available third-party software product. The SAS Web Server, an HTTP server, is based on a Pivotal Web Server.

If you look at running processes, you will see *Pivotal Web Server*, which is the SAS Web Server, and *SpringSource tc Run time*, which is the SAS Web Application Server.

Looking at the configuration directory of the SAS Web Application Servers, you will notice folder names such as SASServer1_1, SASServer2_1, and so forth. The names SASServer*n* are assigned to certain products in your SAS environment. The configuration directory is: **\sas_config_dir\Lev1\Web\WebAppServer**

Figure 2.6 shows the server assignments. Depending on the products you have licensed, you won't have all the servers and with that, probably no sequential numbering.

Figure 2.6: Server Assignments

SASServer 1	Business Intelligence
SASServer 2	Tools
SASServer 3	Performance Management Solutions (General)
SASServer 4	Performance Management Solutions (OLAP)
SASServer 5	Performance Management Solutions (Financial)
SASServer 6	Customer Intelligence Solutions
SASServer 7	Decision Management Solutions
SASServer 8	Risk Management, Fraud & Security Intelligence Solutions
SASServer 9	Performance Management Solutions (Cost & Profitability)
SASServer 10	Performance Management (IT Resource Management)
SASServer 11	Various products (Mid-Tier Support)
SASServer 12	Analytics (Including Visual Analytics & Visual Statistics)
SASServer 13	Data Management Solutions
SASServer 14	Platform Web Services for SAS (Job Scheduler, LSF)
SASServer 15	Data Management Solutions (SAS Data Director)

For details, see SAS Web Application Server Assignments at:
https://go.documentation.sas.com/?docsetId=biwaag&docsetTarget=n1fojaysjal45on1wio1kp d3u8as.htm&docsetVersion=9.4&locale=en

Cache Locator

The SAS Web Application Server uses the cache locator to locate SAS applications that use a data cache for sharing data.

JMS Broker

The JMS Broker is used to send messages between web clients.

SAS Environment Manager

New in SAS 9.4, SAS Environment is a web client that is based on VMware Hyperic, that can be used to monitor and report on your environment. We will talk about this in more detail in Chapter 3.

Java Runtime Environment

There is no need for a JRE in SAS 9.4 as the Java environment is now part of SAS 9.4, compared to prior SAS 9 versions.

A quick note about the Java Runtime Environment, as customers ask about it once in a while. In SAS 9.4, there is no need for a JRE because the Java environment is now part of SAS 9.4, compared to prior SAS 9 versions.

Other web services that you might notice are presented in Table 2.2:

Table 2.2: SAS Web Services

SAS Server Name	VMware Hyperic Service
SAS Environment Manager	Apache Tomcat
SAS Environment Manager Agent	HQ Agent
SAS Web Server	Pivotal Web Server
SAS Web Application Server	SpringSource tc Run time
SAS Web Infrastructure Platform Data Server	PostgreSQL

Knowing the services names helps when it comes to monitoring your environment, so you can recognize what process is actually running.

Wait for it – a link reference ... There is a great article called "SAS 9.4 middle tier architecture: need a map?" which I would like to recommend.
https://blogs.sas.com/content/sgf/2013/09/19/sas-9-4-middle-tier-architecture-need-a-map/

SAS Client Tier

There is not much to say about this tier: it is where your SAS desktop clients run and where your users access SAS web clients via browser.

Data Tier

The data tier "holds" all your data sources. This can be SAS data sets, DBMS tables, multi-dimensional data etc. – simply everything data. SAS offers many options for connecting and accessing data sources, some of which we will cover in Chapter 5, Metadata Library Administration.

Summary

We covered a lot of ground in this chapter. The idea is to provide you with basics, to help you understand the SAS architecture. If you know how it works, and what it includes, SAS administration will be much easier. Here are some good resources for general SAS architecture:

Concluding this chapter, I would like to point out one last find, called "Grand Designs: Why It Pays to Think About Technical Architecture Design Before You Act": http://support.sas.com/resources/papers/proceedings13/475-2013.pdf

When it comes to architecting SAS, or, adding or modifying an already existing SAS environment, be considered and think it through carefully, make sure you have a good plan in place.

Chapter 3: Administration Tools

Introduction

Now that you have the SAS architecture under your belt, you do need some administration tools to support your SAS deployment. In this chapter, I would like to share with you the how to use the four SAS administration tools, namely the SAS Management Console, SAS Environment Manager, SAS Deployment Manager and SAS Web Administration Console. **SAS Management Console** is a desktop client that provides you with control for your SAS deployment to create, manage and administer metadata, such as users, groups and roles, libraries, and more. **SAS Environment Manager** is a web client which can also be used to create, manage and administer metadata. In addition, it is a great monitoring and reporting tool for your SAS environment. It is a great tool for checking on the health of your environment. You can use the **SAS Deployment Manager** to manage your environment in such a way that it enables you to – for example – update your license file, add or remove products, backup, and so on. With the **SAS Web Administration Console**, you can monitor which users are logged on to SAS web applications, view audit reports of logon and logoff activities, manage web-layer authorization, and more.

Why did I choose to write a chapter about SAS admin tools where we have an abundance of documentation available, covering it all? Well, I believe that every newbie needs a sense of direction, info about the value a certain SAS tool provides, and to understand the purpose of the different SAS admin tool available to you. Enjoy the fact that there is one chapter covering the SAS tools that you need versus having to read through all the documentation. In the Appendix for this chapter, you will find some good supporting resources.

Let's get started.

The SAS Jedi: SAS Management Console

Introduction

SAS Management Console is an admin desktop client – which, as the name suggests, is a client that is for admins, and should not be installed on users' machines (except, of course, if they handle certain admin tasks). SAS Management Console enables you to create metadata and manage your SAS environment. As it is a desktop client, it requires that every admin has it installed.

Note: Please consider carefully whether a user needs to have SAS Management Console installed. Always keep in mind that using SAS Management Console provides access to all your assets, such as users, groups, libraries, security, and so forth.

If a user has some admin tasks, for example, creating certain libraries, then make sure you have the appropriate permissions in place to protect the rest of your SAS metadata.

SAS Management Console consists of plug-ins, each of which has a different task. You have a *User Manager* plug-in to create users, groups and roles, a *Library Manager* to create libraries and register tables, and so forth.

The SAS Management Console plug-ins are:
(Resource:
https://go.documentation.sas.com/?docsetId=bisag&docsetTarget=n11i3mqkmnhgu0n1bhm1qmtiep0u.htm&docsetVersion=9.4&locale=en#n0d89q1ljogpuxn16bktpuct9j3x)

Table 3.1 SAS Management Console plug-ins

Plug-in Name	Plug-in Description
Authorization Manager	Define and maintain access rules to control how users and groups can access metadata definitions.
BI Lineage	Identify connections between BI objects in the SAS Folders tree.

Plug-in Name	Plug-in Description
Configuration Manager	View and modify configuration attributes for SAS applications including SAS Information Delivery Portal, SAS Web Report Studio, SAS Financial Management, and SAS Strategic Performance Management.
Data Library Manager	Create and maintain definitions for SAS libraries and database schemas.
Foundation Services Manager	View and modify deployment configurations for infrastructure and extension services that are used by applications such as SAS Information Delivery Portal, SAS BI Dashboard, and SAS Web Report Studio
Map Service Manager	Create and maintain map service definitions that link cubes to Esri ArcGIS map services so that Esri Geographic Information System (GIS) spatial map information can be accessed and returned by an OLAP server when the cubes are queried.
Metadata Manager	Perform administration tasks related to the SAS Metadata Server, including the following: stop, pause, resume, or reset the metadata server check the status of the metadata server and the metadata repositories create and manage metadata repositories back up or restore your metadata repositories analyze and repair metadata
Publishing Framework	Create and maintain definitions for channels, package subscribers, group subscribers, and event subscribers.
Schedule Manager	Create and maintain schedules for running jobs that are created in SAS Data Integration Studio and SAS Web Report Studio.
Server Manager	Perform administration tasks related to SAS servers, including the following: check the status of servers and validate them to ensure that they are configured correctly stop, pause, quiesce, resume, or refresh the SAS object spawner or the SAS/CONNECT spawner, and stop, pause, resume, or quiesce a process on a SAS OLAP Server, SAS Workspace Server, or SAS Stored Process Server connect to the metadata server, to components of SAS Application Servers, to the SAS object spawner, or to the SAS/CONNECT spawner to perform monitoring activities

Plug-in Name	Plug-in Description
User Manager	Create and maintain definitions for users, groups, and roles.

SAS Management Console Connection Profiles

Let's start with logging on to SAS Management Console. You might be thinking, *"why would she cover something so easy? a piece of cake"*. Well, in my experience, many SAS administrators do, in fact, struggle when it comes to the login profile. So, let's take a closer look at it.

When SAS Management Console is started, your first interaction point is a profile that is used to log on: as shown in Figure 3.1.

Figure 3.1: Connection Profile

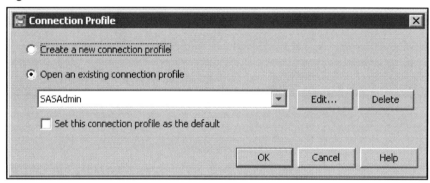

The connection profile is named *SASAdmin*. The *SASAdmin* connection profile is automatically created for you when SAS is installed and configured. You can create new connection profiles, or, share one connection profile amongst several admins. If all the admins in your team share the same administrative responsibilities, then it might make sense to use this one profile. If you do have different profiles, there are ways to deny and grant access to certain functionalities. If this is a singular situation (you are the only admin), in addition to using that profile, send a note to your manager that you need more admins.

If you want to create new profiles, choose the top radio button *Create a new connection profile. (See Figure 3.1.)* Here, I am simply editing the default *SASAdmin* profile to show you what it includes. On the same profile, click *Edit*. The next screenshot shows the actual connection information that you must enter.

Figure 3.2: Connection Information

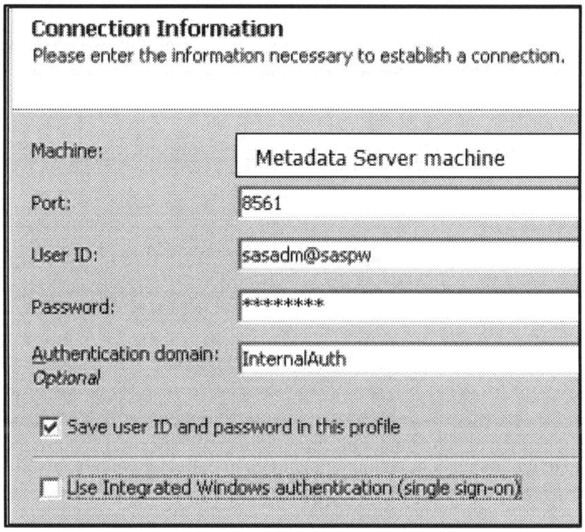

The connection profile includes just that: connection information to the metadata server.

Connection information:

As you manage and administer metadata with SAS Management Console, and, as you know, metadata objects are stored in the metadata's repository, connection information to the metadata server is needed.

- Machine: The machine name of the metadata server machine.

- Port: The default metadata server port is 8561. If you chose another one during the installation of SAS, use that one.

- User ID: The default user ID SAS assigned to the default *SASAdmin* profile is the **SAS internal** administrator user **sasadm@saspw**. This is an unrestricted user who can do everything in metadata, despite any permissions that are set up. It's the user who stands above all. As a best practice, do not share the sasadm@saspw user and password with users/admins who are not supposed to be unrestricted. Consider it a special account with lots of admin power. Limitless access – that is why it's called unrestricted. Whether it makes sense to create different profiles is up to you and really depends on your needs.

- Authentication Domain: The authentication domain shows as *InternalAuth* as sasadm@saspw is an internal user ID. We will cover authentication domains in Chapter 4, when we'll talk about users and groups.

- Save user ID and password: You can choose to save the password and user ID. If you don't check this box, you will be prompted for a user ID and password every time you log on to SAS Management Console.

- You can choose to use single sign-on. Integrated Windows Authentication does not work for SAS internal accounts.

What if you are running in a development, test, production, environment? How does that work? In cases where you have more than one metadata server instance, you will have profiles for each metadata server. Depending on whether the metadata servers run on the same machine or on different machines, the port changes and would have to be 8562 for a Lev2, 8563 for a Lev3, and so on.

Going off track a little here: Using different ports and configuration names (Lev*n*) is necessary so that SAS understands that there are more than one metadata server.

Troubleshooting Connection Profiles: Common Problems and Troubleshooting Tips

What could go wrong with the profile? Why would the logon fail? There are cases where the attempt to log on to SAS Management Console might fail, throwing out one of these annoying error messages … probably first thing in the morning, before you have the chance to sip on your first cup of coffee. But, don't worry, there are easy fixes! The list below gives the error message ("E") followed by its troubleshooting tips ("T").

E: *The application could not log on to the server "machine name:8561". The User ID "userid" or the password is incorrect.*
   T: As the error states, something's up with your user ID or your password. If it is saved in the profile, edit the profile and make sure it is the correct one.

E: *The user "userid" is not authorized to read metadata on server "machine"*
   T: A reason could be that the user who is trying to log on, is not properly registered in metadata. That would be a case for the User Manager plug-in. You can verify by going to the User Manager, making sure that the user actually has a metadata identity, and if yes, the account associated with this metadata user is correct.

E: *The application could not log on to the server <Server name>. The user ID "sasadm@saspw" or the password is incorrect.*
   T: This error can occur when you tried to log on to SAS Management Console for the third time, using the wrong password for the SAS internal admin account sasadm@sapw. Follow the instructions as described below from the SAS Security Administration Guide, available at:
   http://go.documentation.sas.com/?docsetId=mcsecug&docsetTarget=p1hxt5txo0hoapn13 wllie213sbm.htm&docsetVersion=9.4&locale=en

By policy, three consecutive failed attempts to log on with an internal account locks that account for one hour. To immediately unlock a locked internal account:

- In User Manager, select the user whose internal account is locked. Right-click and select Properties.

- Select the Accounts tab. In the confirmation message box, click Yes.

E: *The application could not log on to the server "machine name:8561". No server is available at that port on that machine.*

　T: This error is most likely the result of the metadata server not being started. Check the metadata server service and make sure the server is running. If the metadata server is running, make sure there is no typographical error in the server name, that the port is correct and that no firewall is blocking access to the server's port.

On Windows:

Go to the Services and verify that the metadata server is running. If not, start it. The metadata server is named

`SAS [Config-Lev1] SASMeta - Metadata Server`

where "*Config*" is the name of the configuration directory that you created when SAS was installed. (See chapter 2 for information on configuration directories.)

In my environment, my configuration path is **\sasva\Lev1**, my service shows as:

`SAS [sasva-Lev1] SASMeta - Metadata Server`.

If you prefer to use batch files on Windows versus working with the Services menu, open a DOS command and change the path to **SAS-config-dir/Lev1/SASMeta/MetadataServer**

Then run: `MetadataServer.bat status`

You will see the following output:

`Service_Name:  SAS - [Config-Lev1] SASMeta - Metadata Server`

`        TYPE            :  10  WIN32_OWN_Process`

`        STATE           :  4   RUNNING`

Note: the *TYPE* might look different, depending on what OS you are running.

The *STATE* should show **RUNNING**.

If it doesn't show *RUNNING*, start it with `MetadataServer.bat start`

On UNIX:

You can use the following command to check whether the metadata server is running. Go to **SAS-config-dir/Lev1/SASMeta/MetadataServer** and enter **./sas.servers status**

If your metadata server is running, you'll see:

`server-name server-instance (process-ID) is running`

If it is not running, you can start it by entering **./sas.servers start**

No matter what operating system you are running, if the metadata server cannot be started and there is no easy fix for it, it is best to contact SAS Technical Support.

Working in SAS Management Console

Once you have successfully logged on, you are ready to work with SAS Management Console. As you can see in Figure 3.3, there are different tabs: Plug-ins, Folders and Search.

Figure 3.3: SAS Management Console Interface:

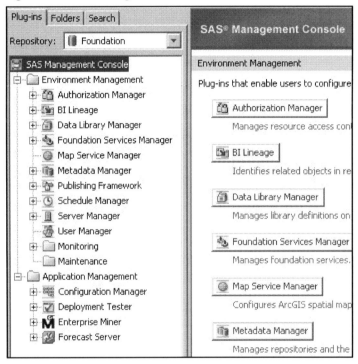

Plug-ins

The Plug-ins enable you to create metadata content, such as users and groups, libraries etc.

I would like to say a few things about the User Manager, Library Manager and Server Manager. Some other plug-ins will be discussed later in this chapter as well.

User Manager

As the name suggests, you use the *User Manager* to administer and maintain your SAS users and groups and roles. We will discuss the User Manager in more detail in Chapter 4, Users and Groups, but for now, the SAS identity that you create in SAS can be operating system users or users that come from an external third-party provider, such as LDAP/AD.

User IDs are used for making access distinctions and track user activity. Eventually, you will want to know who is making requests. It is best practice to create a SAS identity corresponding to the external account for each person who uses the SAS environment.

You can create users interactively, or programmatically.

If you are using LDAP/AD, the SAS bulk load macros can be used to import the users and groups into SAS. The link to the SAS documentation can found in the Appendix.

> **Tip:** SAS admin newbies often ask why they should create users in metadata anyhow, when they already have users on the OS/LDAP. In order to use your SAS environment to its fullest, in order to have control of the "who is doing what in SAS", in order to use SAS security to make sure your SAS environment is locked down appropriately, you must create users in metadata or else, SAS doesn't have anything to report on, to lock down, etc. It is a best practice to build a user and group structure in metadata to – later on – be able to use all the features SAS provides.

Server Manager

Remember when we discussed the SAS servers in Chapter 2, SAS Architecture? These SAS servers are defined in metadata. Using the Server Manager plug-in, you can manage the SAS servers' definitions and define and edit information about server locations and connections.

Under Server Manager, expand SASMeta, expand SASMeta – Logical Server. If you look to the right, you will see that some of the tabs such as Clients – are grayed out, as shown in the following figure:

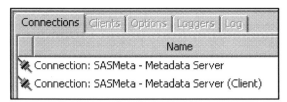

Now, going back to the left side, do a right-click on SASMeta – Metadata Server, Connect. As you can now see on the right side, the tabs become now active, as shown in the following figure:

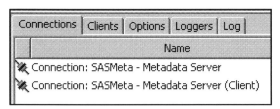

By connecting to the metadata server, it enables you to monitor the activity of the metadata server. It shows:

- Currently connected clients
- Sessions that are active, inactive or terminated

- Performance counters
- Logging messages, at the level that you specify

> **Tip:** Expand the Logical server for the workspace server, stored process server, pooled workspace server, object spawner, connect spawner – all application servers that – in one way or another – start a connection. Then on the right side, highlight the Connection: server_name and do a right-click. A window will appear, offering you a Test Connection. This is a good way to test whether your servers are working correctly, should you ever get into a situation where you must check if a SAS server might be the culprit of a problem.

Library Manager

Libraries are used to register data, so your users can work with it within metadata using SAS clients, such as SAS Enterprise Guide or SAS Studio, as one example. If you do not create libraries and don't register tables, you cannot monitor and report on any user activity, data usage, resources consumed, user processes etc. You can create libraries for different data sources, such as data sets, DBMS (Database Management System) such as Oracle and more.

If you create users and groups in metadata, and you want to set up permissions later on, you need something to actually secure – that is, metadata objects including your libraries. If you don't create libraries in metadata, you can manage access to data through the OS only. With metadata, you can decide which data in an OS folder you want to register. This will make sure you are using the full potential of your SAS environment. We will cover the Library Manager and library and data concepts more in depth in Chapter 5.

When we speak about libraries, SAS *Folders* come into play, which brings us to the next tab in SAS Management Console, the *Folders* tab.

The Folders

The SAS folders are used to store all the SAS metadata objects you and your users create, such as projects created with SAS Enterprise Guide or SAS Enterprise Miner, reports, and stored processes, just all the metadata objects you and your users create.

Folders are provided for individual users, for shared data, for system use, and for specific SAS products. The Folders tab also enables you to export and import metadata (aka Promotion). In the Appendix you will find more information on SAS Folders.

Figure 3.4 is just one example of objects that can be stored in the SAS Folders.

Figure 3.4: SAS Folder Example:

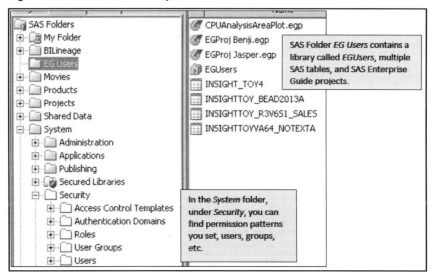

Important: Renaming, deleting, or moving of the folders *System*, *Products*, *Shared Data* or *Users Folders* and their contents can cause your SAS clients to malfunction.

When interacting with folders, be sure to follow the best practices that are provided in the SAS 9.4 System Administration Guide.

Best Practices for Managing SAS Folders
(Resource:
https://go.documentation.sas.com/?cdcId=bicdc&cdcVersion=9.4&docsetId=bisag&docsetTarget=p0sc8uk5ttcvhzn1gfcjhkacwpcu.htm&locale=en)

- Use personal folders for personal content and use shared folders for content that multiple users need to view.

  By default, users cannot view other users' personal folders. Therefore, personal folders should be used for content that needs to be viewed and used only by the owning user. If the content needs to be viewed or used by other users, then it should be placed under the **Shared Data** folder or in a new folder structure that you create under **SAS Folders**.

  To ensure secure and efficient sharing of content, the system administrator should create a folder structure for shared data that meets the needs of the organization. The appropriate permissions can then be assigned to each folder.

- Use folders, instead of custom repositories, to organize content.

  In most cases, folders are the preferred method for organizing content. Custom repositories should be created only when there is an overriding reason to physically segregate repository data sets.

- It is recommended that you not delete or rename the **User Folders** folder, even if you have permission to do so.

  If you have a reason to delete or rename the **User Folders** folder, then you must change the metadata repository configuration to reflect the change.

- Do not delete or rename the home folder or personal folder (**My Folder**) of an active user, even if you have permission to do so.

  As a best practice, do not rename an active user's home folder or personal folder. If you do so, a new (empty) personal folder will be created the next time the user refreshes or logs on to an application that requires the folder. In addition, the contents of the renamed folder will not be visible to the user.

  If you delete an active user's home folder or personal folder, the user will lose any existing personal content, and a new (empty) personal folder will be created the next time the user refreshes or logs on to an application that requires the folder.

- Do not delete or rename the **Products** or **System** folders or their subfolders, even if you have permission to do so.

  Deleting or renaming the **Products** or **System** folders or their subfolders could cause erroneous or unexpected behavior in client applications or solutions.

- Use caution when renaming the **Shared Data** folder.

  Renaming the **Shared Data** folder can affect associations and references to objects that are stored in this folder or its subfolders.

We will talk more about the SAS folders in Chapter 5.

> **Note:** The Folders in SAS Management Console have nothing to do with operating system folders. The operating systems cannot see, nor understand, the folders in SAS Management Console. Same if you look at it the other way around. SAS Folders don't know about the Operating System folders. These two are totally independent. You can create a SAS folder structure based on what you set up on the OS though.

The Search tab

The third tab on the SAS Management Console is the Search tab:

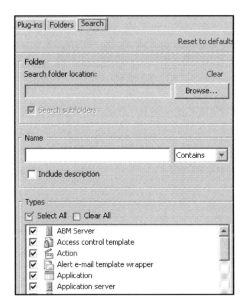

Which is, well, self-explanatory. You can search for objects in your metadata. Check out Using Search for details and examples: Go to the menu, *Help*, *Help on Search*.

SAS Management Console Debugging

SAS Management Console writes a log file per default, which is called **SASMCErrorLog.txt**. The log file can be found at these locations:

Windows:
C:\Users*your-user-ID*\AppData\Roaming\SAS\SASManagementConsole\9.*x*\ , or, depending on the Windows flavor you are running, at C:\Documents and Settings*user-ID*\Application Data\SAS\SASManagementConsole\9.*x*\ or,
C:\Users\sas\AppData\Roaming\SAS\SASManagementConsole\9.4

UNIX and Linux:
~user's-home-dir/SAS/SASManagementConsole/9.x/

If you did not accept the default during the SAS configuration, make sure you look for the right folder name.

If the default logging information does not suffice for troubleshooting, you can enable debugging. To do so, follow these steps:

1. On Windows, go to C:\Program Files\SAS\SASManagementConsole\9.*x*.; on Unix/Linux, go to *SASHOME*/SASManagementConsole/9.*x*
2. Edit the file **sasmc.ini**
3. Look for the entry **MainClass=com.sas.console.visuals.MainConsole**

4. Add the following at the end of that line: **-debug -serverlog**
   The entry should now look like:
   MainClass=com.sas.console.visuals.MainConsole -debug -serverlog

5. Open SAS Management Console and then close it.

The now created log file includes more detailed logging information. Should the log be empty, or, does not include any hints for the issue, contact SAS Technical Support for further troubleshooting.

Redirecting Local Files

If you want your SAS Management Console files (log files, application default files, and connection profiles) on the server rather than on your local client, you can redirect the files by following these steps:

1. Close SAS Management Console on the local host.
2. Create the path and directory for the client files on the server.
3. Edit the file sasmc.ini and add the following Java argument:
   JavaArgs_xx=-Dsas.appdatapath="new_path"
   xx is the next available Java argument number, and **new_path** is a fully qualified path to the new directory.
4. The changes take effect when SAS Management Console is started.

Here is an example of a redirection path. Let's assume my machine name is **Anja171**. The path I would create on the server would be something like:

JavaArgs_xx=-Dsas.appdatapath="\\server\SASMCclientFiles\Anja171"

The machine name at the end makes sense because if all admins, or users using SAS Management Console, write their files to the server, you want to make sure that everyone has their own dedicated folder, to make sure the files won't overwrite each other.

Why would you want to redirect SAS Management Console files?
Typically, it gives you better control of the files. For example, if you do have users who use SAS Management Console, you might want to make sure that the configuration files cannot be changed. Or, you simply want to have your local SAS Management Console files "globally" available. I have not come across many situations where customers redirected the local SAS Management Console files. However, I consider it as a good-to-know.

This concludes our introduction to SAS Management Console.

SAS Environment Manager

Monitoring your SAS Environment

There are many tools that can be used to monitor the SAS environment, such as nmon for UNIX and Linux, or perfmon for Windows, and monitoring tools from Tivoli and Computer

Associates, and so on, but in this chapter, we solely focus on the SAS monitoring tool called SAS Environment Manager. This admin tool enables you to monitor how SAS is being used, with the hardware resources SAS is running on. In addition to the monitoring and reporting functionality, SAS Environment Manager provides many of the tasks and functionalities that you have available in SAS Management Console. It also has a User Manager, a Library Manager, etc.

The most obvious difference between SAS Management Console and SAS Environment Manager is that one is a desktop client, the other is a web client. Where SAS Management Console has to be installed on the desktops, or, handled on the server, SAS Environment Manager is a web client, which makes it easy to access from everywhere.

The Environment Manager is great for checking your SAS environment's vital signs. You know, the typical: pulse, body temperature, breathing rate (and while you are at it, your blood pressure). Or, in computing terms:

- How busy are the CPUs?
- Is there enough bandwidth to support all concurrent sessions?
- Is there enough memory?
- Are there any error messages in the server logs?

You want to ensure that your infrastructure is set up to support all the SAS workloads and I/O profiles in your environment.

Best Practices for Monitoring

When it comes to recommendations, or best practices for what might be useful to monitor, an important part here is to consider working with your users: what are their needs, do they see any problems performance vice, are there situation where things just freeze - you know, the typical admin headaches.

Areas to monitor:

- **How busy are the CPUs?** If they are above 80% for long periods of time and future growth is anticipated, you need to start planning to increase the number of cores.

- **How much free memory is available?** If the amount of free memory goes down to 0 and you are seeing paging or swapping and your paging daemons are showing pressure (or your SAS users are expressing concerns about how long their SAS applications are taking), then the system has run out of memory. If this happens for only a few minutes, you should start planning to add more RAM. If this happens for longer periods of time and these times are during peak SAS usage, you need to increase the amount of RAM in your system.

- **How much free space is there in the various file systems being used by SAS?** When file systems start to reach 90+% full, there is overhead to finding free space for new writes. You should work with your SAS users to determine whether there are any SAS data files that can be archived to slower storage or tape.

- **What is the I/O throughput?** SAS recommends a minimum of 100 MB/second/core I/O throughput. Ensuring that you can achieve this I/O throughput is part of the initial hardware infrastructure setup and configuration. Note that this I/O throughput rate is a minimum; your SAS users (or at least your SAS production applications) might need more I/O throughput.

  Monitoring the values of reads and writes to all SAS file systems is a must. You should keep the numbers from the initial configuration as baseline values. Over time, compare your new I/O throughput values to determine whether you are seeing performance degradation in any of the file systems. From SAS customer experience, the temporary SAS file systems (WORK and UTILLOC) are the ones that see the most performance degradation.

- **Are you experiencing any WAIT states?** WAIT states means that there are not enough computer resources to support the SAS sessions. If you see WAIT states of 10+% for a process and there are plenty of CPU and memory resources, then you need to monitor the I/O subsystem infrastructure. Note that this infrastructure is more than the disks in the storage device that stores the SAS data files. It includes the fiber adapters out the front of the storage device; any switches or HBAs (host bus adapters); the network connecting the storage device to the CPU; and the network adapters that are part of the CPUs. Your I/O throughput is only as fast as the slowest component of your I/O subsystem infrastructure.

- **Monitor SAS logs?** If your SAS users are seeing different behavior with their current SAS jobs compared to several weeks or months ago, then you need to review the SAS logs from the runs in question to see why the times have changed. Have the data volumes being processed increased? Have more SAS steps been added to recent versions of the SAS job, thereby making them run longer? Are there any ERRORs in the SAS jobs (file system full or out of memory ERRORs)?

- **How long are your production runs taking?** Production jobs generally have an SLA (service level agreement) associated with them. You need to monitor how long these SAS jobs are taking. If you are reaching the SLA upper limit, determine what can be done to improve the performance of the SAS jobs. If you are not seeing any potential bottlenecks from your hardware infrastructure, you might need to work with your SAS application developer to determine whether the SAS jobs can be reengineered to meet the SLA requirements. If the reengineering means running more SAS jobs simultaneously, then you need to validate that you have enough hardware resources (CPU, memory, I/O throughput, and disk space) to support the additional SAS jobs.

- **What users and applications are connecting to the system?** Monitor user and network application audit reports to see what users and applications are connecting to the system. Remove any users who have not connected to the system recently.

In the following, you will learn how you can use SAS Environment Manager to check the health of your system and get informed if things might turn into the "be careful" stage.

A quick note about the SAS Environment Manager services and relevant web services.

On windows, the processes are:

SAS[machine_name-Lev1] SAS Environment Manager

SAS[machine_name-Lev1] SAS Environment Manager Agent

SAS[machine_name-Lev1] Web Infrastructure Platform Data Server

On UNIX, the agent process is called *hq-agent* and the server process is *hq-server*. The location is:
SAS_config/Web/**SASEnvironmentManager**/agent-5.8.0-EE/bin/

SAS_config/Web/**SASEnvironmentManager**/server-5.8.0-EE\bin

The SAS Environment Manager agent is a process that runs on the middle tier and server tier in your SAS environment. The agent's task is it to gather information for its machine, such as gathering metrics, information about data usage, performance and more.

When you start working with SAS Environment metrics to monitor resources, you will notice service names such as Apache, Pivotal etc. The reason is that SAS Environment Manager is based on VMware's Hyperic. These service names are not the same then what has been created during the SAS installation and configuration. To make the monitoring easier, Table 3.2 is a list of SAS server names and their respective Hyperic names.

Table 3.2: SAS server names and their respective Hyperic names.

SAS Server Name	VMware Hyperic Service
SAS Environment Manager	Apache Tomcat
SAS Environment Manager Agent	HQ Agent
SAS Web Server	Pivotal Web Server
SAS Web Application Server	SpringSource tc Run time
SAS Web Infrastructure Platform Data Server	PostgreSQL
SAS JMS Broker	ActiveMQ

A common question is whether the open-source plugins that are available for VMware Hyperic, can be used. These plugins are not supported by SAS Environment Manager.

Another question that comes up occasionally is if one SAS Environment Manager can be used to monitor several metadata server environments (such as dev, test, prod for example).

This depends on your SAS Environment Manager version and thus on the SAS 9.4 version that you are running. Starting with SAS 9.4 M3, it is possible to monitor different environments with one SAS Environment Manager instance. Prior to SAS 9.4 M3, each metadata server deployment required its own SAS Environment Manager instance.

Before we dig into the actual SAS Environment Manager features, we'll have to have a word about the SAS Environment Manager users and groups.

Users, Groups and SAS Environment Manager

Remember when we talked metadata in Chapter 2 – Architecture? And when we talked about the creation of users and groups in metadata using SAS Management Console, User Manager – in this chapter? If you paid close attention, it might not come as a surprise that the users using SAS Environment Manager, too, must exist in metadata.

Important here is to also know that the users using SAS Environment Manager must be members of specific groups, which are:

- SAS Environment Manager Super Users, or
- SAS Environment Manager Guests, or
- SAS Environment Manager App Server Tier Users

If you run SAS Environment Manager version 2.4 and higher and you enabled the SAS Environment Manager Data Mart Performance and Usage Reporting (see https://blogs.sas.com/content/sgf/2014/11/26/sas-environment-manager-data-mart-the-heart-of-the-service-management-architecture/) functionality, two additional groups are being added:

- SAS Environment Manager Data Mart Users
- SAS Environment Manager Data Mart Administrators

When SAS is installed and configured, SAS assigns certain users to these groups.

For example, the SAS unrestricted admin user sasadm@saspw is member of the SAS Environment Manager Super User group.

A service account called sasevs@saspw is, just as the unrestricted admin user sasadm@saspw, an internal SAS user that is automatically created during the SAS install. This user is a member of the *SAS_EV_AppServer_Tier* (SAS Environment Manager App Server Tier Users) and *SAS_EV_Guest* (SAS Environment Manager Guests) groups in SAS metadata. The purpose of this account is to be a communicator between the SAS Environment Manager agent and SAS Environment Manager server and to communicate with the metadata server.

Starting SAS Environment Manager

SAS Environment Manager is accessed via web browser, using the following link:

http://machinename.com:7080/

where "*machinename*" is the name of your middle tier machine. Port **7080** is the default port used during the SAS deployment. SAS Environment Manager can be configured for HTTPS, which would then be port **7443**.

If you are unsure whether the default port was used, or, what the exact link is, you can take a look at the *instructions.html file*. This file is stored at:
`SAS-config-dir/Lev1/Documents/Instructions.html`.
The *instructions.html* file is created after your SAS environment has been installed and

configured; it includes important information about your install and configuration, such as paths, ports used, links, default users created etc. It can generally be helpful to look up information about your SAS configuration.

When you open the file, go to the *SAS Environment Manager Configuration*.

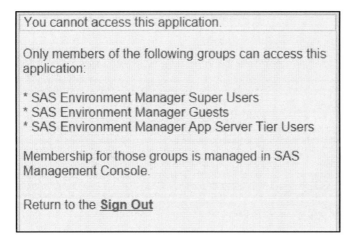

Under *SAS Environment Manager Web Console*, you'll find the link to start the tool, as shown in the following screenshot:

SAS Environment Manager Configuration	
SAS Environment Manager Name	machine_name.na.xxx.com
SAS Environment Manager Port Name	7080
SAS Environment Manager Secure Port Name	7443
SAS Environment Manager Home Dir	C:\SAS\Config\Lev1\Web\SASEnvironmentManager\server-5.8.0-EE
SAS Environment Manager Administrator Name	sasadm@saspw
SAS Environment Manager Administrator Email Address	email@xxx.com
SAS Environment Manager Database Type	PostgreSQL
SAS Environment Manager Database Server	machine_name.na.xxx.com
SAS Environment Manager Database Server Port Name	9432
SAS Environment Manager Database Server Name	EVManager
SAS Environment Manager Web Console	http://machine_name.xxx.com:7080/
Log directory	C:\SAS\Config\Lev1\Web\SASEnvironmentManager\server-5.8.0-EE\logs

When you start SAS Environment Manager, you will now be prompted for user ID and password. When you log on to SAS Environment Manager for the first time, use the internal unrestricted SAS admin ID, sasadm@saspw.

It happens sometimes that a user (SAS admin or whoever can use SAS Environment Manager) gets an error when logging on to SAS Environment Manager. The error is:

```
You cannot access this application.

Only members of the following groups can access this
application:

* SAS Environment Manager Super Users
* SAS Environment Manager Guests
* SAS Environment Manager App Server Tier Users

Membership for those groups is managed in SAS
Management Console.

Return to the Sign Out
```

Remember when I just talked about the SAS Environment Manager groups? (you better, it was just a minute ago). The error occurs because the user is not a member of one of the SAS Environment Manager groups.

The problem is that the user ID that you are using to log on to SAS Environment Manager is not a member of one of the mandatory SAS Environment Manager metadata groups.

Another common error is:

This page can't be displayed

- Make sure the web address http://machine_name:7081 is correct

If this error occurs, make sure the machine name, the port and / or the spelling is correct. In this case, the port I am using is 7081 instead of 7080. If you are unsure, take a look at the *instructions.html* file to find the correct link.

After a successful log on, you are "landing" on the dashboard.

The Dashboard

Once you are logged on to SAS Environment Manager, your "landing page" is the so-called *Dashboard*. The Dashboard shows data from monitored resources. Using pre-defined portlets, you can set up the resources and services that you like to monitor. The Dashboard information is an ad hoc info, which means, you are going into SAS Environment Manager and are actively looking at your resources. Another non-interactive way of monitoring resources is by setting up alerts. Customers usually use a mix of both.

Looking at the Dashboard, you will notice the following in the left upper corner: *Select a Dashboard* as shown in Figure 3.5.

Figure 3.5: Dashboard

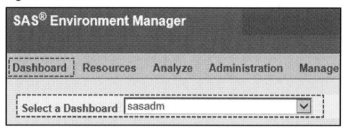

The *sasadm* is the name of the Dashboard, which is chosen per default. You also have other different dashboards available by default:

- **Guest Role.** I would say that the name of the guest role dashboard is self-explanatory: it's a dashboard that guest users can use. Maybe you have users who are interested in keeping an eye on the WORK directory. Or you could use the Guest Role dashboard to show the higher ups that the CPUs are really way too busy, and the disk space way too small, highlighting and proving the necessity for new hardware resources. So, you could say, the Guest dashboard can be used for resource-interested-non-administrators.

- **SAS App Tier Role Dashboard.** This dashboard is used to monitor certain SAS servers. A scenario where using this Dashboard might make sense is if you have a group of admins who support different aspects of SAS. Some admins might be solely focused on the availability of the SAS servers, such as SAS metadata server or SAS object spawner, for example.

- **Super User Role.** The Super User Role dashboard is just that: a dashboard for super users. I would say that the way you define the term Super User is entirely up to you. There are companies who use the term Super User for power users, or regular users, other use it to solely categorize SAS admins. I think the best way to put it: use the already existing Dashboards as you please, or, create your own custom dashboard.

Many folks new to SAS administration have difficulties exploring SAS Environment Manager, and some of the things provided do not seem clear. For that reason, I won't cover every detail about the menu items, but select the ones I realize seem to be more difficult to grasp. We'll start off by talking about the Dashboard and then cover Resources and Analyze.

Creating Custom Dashboards

I realize that many admins don't know about this, so I would like to take this opportunity and guide you through the creation of a custom dashboard. Note, though, that "Customize" here does not mean customizing the actual dashboard with the resources that you want to monitor. It means to actually create a new dashboard itself that you can customize for yourself, or, customize for a group of admins. For example, see Figure 3.6 for a custom dashboard called *Benji Role.*

Figure 3.6: Custom Dashboard

How did we get here? Benji is one of my admins. He needs a dashboard to view escalations and create escalation schemas, and also to monitor resources. To create your own dashboard, choose the **Manage** menu, then **Authentication/Authorization** as section, and click *New Role*. The result is shown in Figure 3.7.

Figure 3.7: Creating a dashboard.

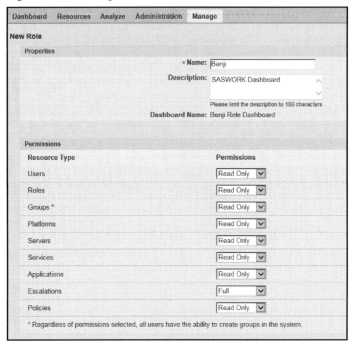

In the Name field, name your dashboard. The *Permissions* section enables you to define which resources and components the user should have access to. Benji has Read Only on all resources except the Escalations, where he has full permissions.

Click *OK* to save the newly created Dashboard.

In the menu, click *Dashboard*, and *Select a Dashboard* to see the Benji Dashboard. This scenario for creating a custom dashboard as described, assumes that user Benji is a member of one of the SAS Environment Manager groups mentioned previously. If he is not a member yet, verify in SAS Management Console to make sure the user is in fact a member of described groups.

Working with the Dashboard page

SAS provides you with portlets that are used to set up your dashboard. You can create your dashboard so that it shows you all the monitoring information that are important to you. The Dashboard is divided into two columns as shown in Figure 3.8.

Figure 3.8: Dashboard Layout

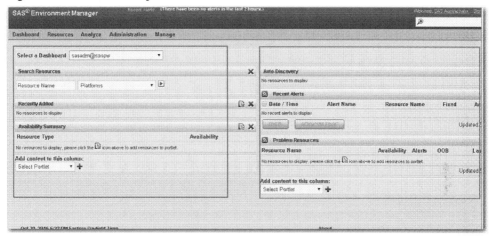

In the left side of the dashboard, you can edit the **Availability Summaries**. The summary portlets are used to monitor the availability of your SAS environment and its components. You can choose from the following options: Available, Unavailable or Undetermined.

Right column: Metrics and Recent Alerts

The portlets available on that side right side of the dashboard are used to monitor the environment, and to see alerts that might have occurred (later on, we will go through an example for creating alerts).

Best Practice and Advice

Working with many customers, and destroying multiple of my own SAS environments with my down-and-dirty-test-and-kill practice, I would like to say:

Do not overpack your dashboards, and, do not go wild with the number of dashboards you might create. If your dashboard is so loaded with information that is so long and big that you must scroll through it for half an hour to actually find what you are looking for, or, if you create 50 dashboards for 2 admins, it's a bit of an overload. There is no limitation of dashboards or limitation of information a dashboard can have, but it's a matter of common sense, desired response times when looking for information, and non-cluttered environments, if you know what I mean. As for the number of dashboards and the question of whether you want to create custom ones or not, be considered, do a proper planning.

Think about the personas that you have created in SAS Management Console, User Manager – the users and groups. Then decide which of these groups might need access to SAS Environment Manager, considering whether the pre-existent dashboards can be used, or, if custom dashboards would make sense. If you decide to create custom dashboards, consider the resources that you want to monitor. If two admins need to monitor all SAS servers in your environment, it might not make sense to create two custom dashboards, but to either use the SAS App Tier Role Dashboard, or, create one custom dashboard that is shared amongst those two SAS administrators. Whatever you decide, remember to make the users and/or groups a member of any of the SAS Environment Manager groups or Role.

I sometimes get the question if dashboards could be created based on resources to monitor, for example, one dashboard for Alerts on all important SAS servers and services, one Dashboard for user interactions etc. The answer is: probably, but does it make sense? With lots of fantasy and a great deal of adventure, I could imagine the following scenario: Big Grid environment (we did not want to cover any add-on SAS deployments, but it's a good example to be used here), 20 machines. You want to monitor the entire Grid of course but would also want to monitor each individual machine in the Grid in a more secluded way. That means, you would end up with twenty-one Dashboards: twenty for each individual machine and one for the entire Grid together. Doesn't sound like a very reasonable approach, does it? So, let me change my answer: probably, but it does not make sense.

Now that we've covered Dashboards, let's move on to the other items on the menu bar.

The Menu Bar

Below is a screenshot of the SAS Environment Manager menu bar.

Here's what each item is:

Menu Bar Item	Meaning
Dashboard	We covered that.
Resources	Monitoring your SAS services, processes
Analyze	Analyzing environment activities
Administration	Backup, User Manager, Libraries, SAS Folders, permissions
Manage	Create dashboards and synchronize users. We covered that as well.

Resources Menu

To see every process running in your SAS Environment, use the *Resources* feature in Environment manager. Click *Resources* and then *Browse* as shown in Figure 3.9.

Figure 3.9: Resources Menu

Once you choose the Resource menu, this is what you'll see the options shown in Figure 3.10.

Figure 3.10: Looking up resources

The Platforms, Servers and Services options list every process that is running in your SAS environment, or, or used by your SAS environment. To check it out, click Servers in the menu and enter *Metadata Server* in the Search field. It will list the metadata server in your environment, and if you click on it, you are diving into the wonderful world of monitoring. What you see here is the default view. There are many other resources that you can choose for viewing. Figure 3.11, is a screenshot from my environment.

Figure 3.11: Metadata Server indicators

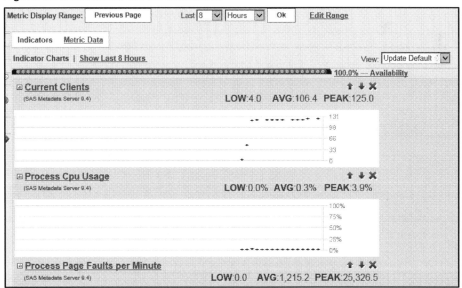

The green dots near the top of Figure 3.14 indicate that everything is OK and up and running. You can see that the time frame defaults to 8 hours. You can change the view to certain dates, or choose specific time frames, such as 120 hours, 120 days etc. As a best practice, you might want to be thoughtful when choosing time frames, because the bigger the time span, the more "cluttered" the view becomes. What you see in this Figure 3.14 are indicators. If you click the Metric *Data*, you get some nice graphs.

Good-To-Know

Sometimes when you look at a resource, for example the SAS servers, you might see that the services show as down, as shown in by the exclamation marks on the right side of Figure 3.12.

Figure 3.12: SAS Server Resource Example

Server ▾	Server Type	Description	Availability
SASBI.demo.sas.com SASMeta - Metadata Server	SAS Metadata Server 9.4	SAS [Config-Lev1] SASMeta - Metadata Server @ C:\SAS\Config\Lev1\SASMeta\MetadataServer	⊕
SASBI.demo.sas.com SASApp - OLAP Server	SAS OLAP Server 9.4	SAS [Config-Lev1] SASApp - OLAP Server @ C:\SAS\Config\Lev1\SASApp\OLAPServer	⊕
SASBI.demo.sas.com Object Spawner - sasbi	SAS Object Spawner 9.4	SAS [Config-Lev1] Object Spawner @ C:\SAS\Config\Lev1\ObjectSpawner	⊕

Yet, you know for a fact that all SAS servers are up and running, check out Problem Note 57076: SAS® Environment Manager Shows Resources as Being Down, available at: http://support.sas.com/kb/57/076.html

Now let's have a closer look at the Alerts and the Reports, as this is one of the main concerns SAS administrators have.

Analyze Menu

To access the alert center in Environment manager, select *Analyze* from the main menu bar and then *Alert Center* as shown in Figure 3.13.

Figure 3.13: Analyze Menu

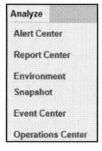

Alert Center

Alerts are very important and helpful when working with any environment, whether it is SAS or not SAS, getting instant notification if something's up, not going right, is very helpful for administrators. Especially since you might catch problems before your users even encounter any problems.

An example that comes to mind is memory. If you are being alerted if – let's say – 80% of the memory is used, you can do something about it and prevent that users hit a problem because all of a sudden, no memory is left for SAS requests. If you hit a memory problem, one of the things that you could check for are services, such as SAS Enterprise Guide sessions that might run unnecessarily, or, processes that might hang and just use up resources.

When you click on the *Alert Center* menu, you'll see an overview for pre-built alerts that come with SAS.

You can either adjust the already existing alerts, or, you can create your own alert definitions. Examples for alerting could be work space, disk space and the like. If you click Definitions as shown in Figure 3.14, you can see a detailed list. Clicking on any alert will show you the alert configuration.

Figure 3.14: Definitions Tab

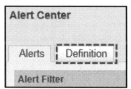

When you create your own Alerts, you can define who has to be alerted. This setting is easy to overlook. e If you, too, don't see it at first, *Notify User* is at the bottom of the page – the fine print. (See Figure 3.15.) Select *Notify Users*, and then select Add to List.

Figure 3.15: Notify Users

There are some great blogs and information available. for you. Here is one example: SAS Environment Manager: Details on Alerting, available at:
https://blogs.sas.com/content/sgf/2015/11/05/sas-environment-manager-details-on-alerting/

More can be found in the Appendix.

Report Center

Sticking with the Analyze menu, let's talk briefly about the Report Center. Not about what it does and how it works, but rather about how you get there. The Report Center must be initialized and will not be available unless you do so. When you click the Report Center the first time, you might get a note such as:

```
Report Center is currently unavailable. Service Architecture has not
been initialized.
```

Don't worry, this is not an error. It is just simply an informative note that you must take some further steps.
For the hardcopy readers: In your SAS environment, go to
`Lev1\Web\SASEnvironmentManager\emi-framework` and look for a PDF file called
SAS_Environment_Manager_Service_Architecture_Quickstart. It provides the steps needed to initialize.

Good Reads on Report Center

More resources can be found in the Appendix.

Administration Menu

With the Administration menu, you can create the following:

- Folders and objects
- Authorization controls
- Users and groups
- Libraries
- Database server definitions
- SAS content backups

As you can see, many of the functionalities that you have in SAS Environment Manager are available in SAS Management Console as well, such as Users and groups, libraries and more. You can restrict the modules shown in the SAS Administration menu by using metadata role capabilities (either in SAS Management Console or SAS Environment Manager. In this example, I am using SAS Management Console). Removing a capability prevents the module from appearing in the Administration side menu. Start SAS Management Console and select the *User Manager* plug-in. Look for the role called *Management Console: Content Management* and open the properties. Select the Capabilities tab. Expand *SAS Management Console 9.4*, go to *Plug-ins* to modify the capabilities as needed.

To show you an example. The screenshot below shows that the Authorization Manager, Data Library Manager, Folder View, Search View and User Manager are available to me:

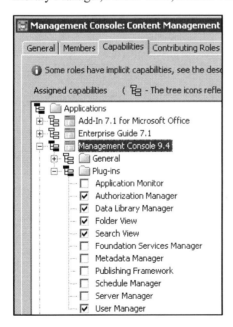

> **Note:** Identities created or modified in SAS Management Console appear in SAS Environment Manager after synchronization. Identities created in SAS Environment Manager appear in SAS Management Console with no further interaction.

Best Practices for Monitoring

When it comes to recommendations, or best practices for what might be useful to monitor, an important part here is to consider working with your users. What are their needs? Do they see any problems with performance? Are there situation where things just freeze? In her paper, *Ensuring that Your SAS® Infrastructure Is Able to Meet Your SAS Users' Demands*, Margaret Crevar shared some of the following best practices, which I have excerpted below (*Ensuring that Your SAS® Infrastructure Is Able to Meet Your SAS Users' Demands"* by Margaret Crevar. SAS Global Forum 2016 Proceedings. Copyright © 2016 by SAS Institute Inc., Cary, NC, USA. All Rights Reserved. Reproduced with permission of SAS Institute Inc., Cary, NC"):

- **How busy are the CPUs?** If they are above 80% for long periods of time and future growth is anticipated, you need to start planning to increase the number of cores.

- **How much free memory is available?** If the amount of free memory goes down to 0 and you are seeing paging or swapping and your paging daemons are showing pressure (or your SAS users are expressing concerns about how long their SAS applications are taking), then the system has run out of memory. If this happens for only a few minutes, you should start planning to add more RAM. If this happens for longer periods of time and these times are during peak SAS usage, you need to increase the amount of RAM in your system.

- **How much free space is there in the various file systems being used by SAS?** When file systems start to reach 90+% full, there is overhead to finding free space for new writes. You should work with your SAS users to determine whether there are any SAS data files that can be archived to slower storage or tape.

- **What is the I/O throughput?** SAS recommends a minimum of 100 MB/second/core I/O throughput. Ensuring that you can achieve this I/O throughput is part of the initial hardware infrastructure setup and configuration. Note that this I/O throughput rate is a minimum; your SAS users (or at least your SAS production applications) might need more I/O throughput.
  Monitoring the values of reads and writes to all SAS file systems is a must. You should keep the numbers from the initial configuration as baseline values. Over time, compare your new I/O throughput values to determine whether you are seeing performance degradation in any of the file systems. From SAS customer experience, the temporary SAS file systems (WORK and UTILLOC) are the ones that see the most performance degradation.

- **Are you experiencing any WAIT states?** WAIT states means that there are not enough computer resources to support the SAS sessions. If you see WAIT states of 10+% for a process and there are plenty of CPU and memory resources, then you need to monitor the I/O subsystem infrastructure. Note that this infrastructure is more than the disks in the storage device that stores the SAS data files. It includes the fiber adapters out the front of the storage device; any switches or HBAs (host bus adapters); the network connecting the storage device to the CPU; and the network adapters that are part of the CPUs. Your I/O throughput is only as fast as the slowest component of your I/O subsystem infrastructure.

- **Monitor SAS logs?** If your SAS users are seeing different behavior with their current SAS jobs compared to several weeks or months ago, then you need to review the SAS logs from the runs in question to see why the times have changed. Have the data volumes being processed increased? Have more SAS steps been added to recent versions of the SAS job, thereby making them run longer? Are there any ERRORs in the SAS jobs (file system full or out of memory ERRORs)?

- **How long are your production runs taking?** Production jobs generally have an SLA (service level agreement) associated with them. You need to monitor how long these SAS jobs are taking. If you are reaching the SLA upper limit, determine what can be done to improve the performance of the SAS jobs. If you are not seeing any potential bottlenecks from your hardware infrastructure, you might need to work with your SAS application developer to determine whether the SAS jobs can be reengineered to meet the SLA requirements. If the reengineering means running more SAS jobs simultaneously, then you need to validate that you have enough hardware resources (CPU, memory, I/O throughput, and disk space) to support the additional SAS jobs.

- **What users and applications are connecting to the system?** Monitor user and network application audit reports to see what users and applications are connecting to the system. Remove any users who have not connected to the system recently.

SAS Management Console or SAS Environment Manager?

The question of whether to use Management Console or Environment Manager comes up so frequently that I believe this is a good place to address it, now that you are familiar with both. First, let's consider access. One obvious difference is that one is a desktop client and one is a web client.

Convenience-wise SAS Environment Manager might have the lead because it can be accessed from everywhere you have internet. SAS Management Console must be installed on the administrators' desktop or has to be accessed via remote desktop, if you want to have easy access to it. But what about functionality?

Currently, you do not have all functionalities available in SAS Environment Manager that you have in SAS Management Console.

You can use either tool to maintain and administer SAS servers, monitor a SAS Grid environment, administer SAS folders (create, view etc.), create and maintain users, groups and roles, run a backup, create and maintain libraries. The big difference is the ability to run precise and detailed reports on your environment using SAS Environment; a feature SAS Management Console does not have.

The SAS 9.4 System Administration Guide has a nice table as shown below where the different functionalities are compared, as shown in the following table. Resource: https://go.documentation.sas.com/?docsetId=bisag&docsetTarget=p13sfvw3fabjcwn16a8nf7c q34yh.htm&docsetVersion=9.4&locale=en

Table 3.3 Comparison of SAS Management Console and the Current Version of SAS Environment Manager

Administration Task	Available in SAS Environment Manager?	Available in SAS Management Console?
Start, stop, and restart the SAS Web Application Server; and start, stop, and reload web applications.	✓	
View metrics on the availability, performance, utilization, resource consumption, and throughput of server machines on the middle tier and the SAS server tier. Set up alerts based on these metrics.	✓	
Use reporting tools to obtain a comprehensive view of the performance and status of your SAS environment and its resources.	✓2	
Start servers on the SAS server tier.	✓	
Pause, resume, quiesce, and stop servers on the SAS server tier; and view the status of server processes on the SAS server tier	✓	✓
View events of a specified level from server log files.	✓	✓
View server logs and dynamically change logging levels.		✓
Validate servers on the SAS server tier and run the Deployment Tester.		✓
Schedule, configure, monitor, and perform integrated backups of your SAS content across multiple tiers and machines.	✓3	
Back up and restore the metadata server, and create and administer metadata repositories.		✓
Monitor the operation of grids, and administer grid hosts, queues, and jobs.	✓3	✓
Schedule flows to run on a scheduling server.		✓
Browse the contents of SAS folders, view and update properties of folders and objects, and rename and delete objects.	✓	✓
Create, rename, and delete SAS folders.	✓1	✓
Create and modify metadata definitions for users, groups, and roles; and manage memberships, logins, and internal accounts.	✓2	✓
Define metadata access rules, and create and update access control templates (ACTs).	✓1	✓
Browse any type of library or server that has been defined in SAS metadata.	✓3	✓

Administration Task	Available in SAS Environment Manager?	Available in SAS Management Console?
Create and modify metadata definitions for Base SAS libraries, SAS LASR Analytic Server libraries, and SAS LASR Analytic Servers.		
Create and modify metadata definitions for other types of SAS libraries and servers.		✓
Create and modify metadata definitions for database schemas, map services, servers, stored processes, publication channels, and subscribers.		✓
Display lineage information.		✓
Promote (export and import), copy, and paste metadata.		✓
View and modify configuration attributes for SAS applications, and view and modify deployment configurations for infrastructure and extension services that are used by these applications.		✓

1 This functionality was added with the first and second maintenance releases for SAS 9.4.

2 This functionality was added in release 2.4 of SAS Environment Manager.

3 This functionality was added with SAS 9.4M3.

In summary, I would say that SAS Environment Manager is a pretty powerful tool for your SAS environment. The best advice I can give you? Become familiar with the basics, and then do the real trial and error.

SAS Deployment Manager

This tool is a cross-platform swiss army knife. It lets you configure products, applying hot fixes, update metadata, uninstalling SAS software, update host name references, update existing configurations and much more, as shown in Figure 3.16.

Figure 3.16: SAS Deployment Manager Tasks

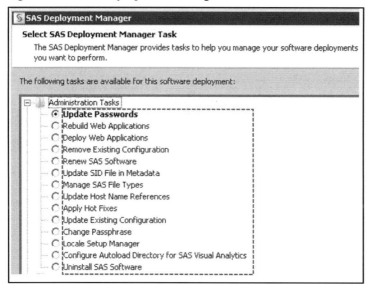

Start the Deployment Manager by running sasdm.exe on Windows and sasdm.sh on UNIX. The executable is in: **SAS-installation-directory\SASDeploymentManager\9.4**

Let's talk about some of the tasks that you can do with itDeployment Manager.

Update Passwords

This task might be a bit confusing as because it sounds like you can update just any password. This is not true. In fact, this option enables you to change passwords for service accounts only. An example for service accounts could be sasevs@saspw or sasadm@saspw. The service accounts you see depend on the products you have installed and configured. During the process of updating SAS service accounts, you will be prompted for a password. This is the password for the user under which the Deployment Manager is running under (the password for the user making the change).

An example for a list of users you can see is shown in Figure 3.17.

Figure 3.17: Example User ID List

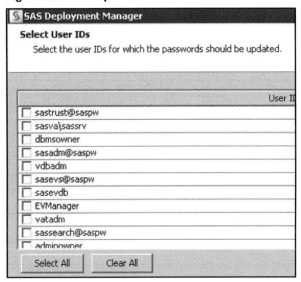

Rebuild Web Applications / Deploy Web Applications

The SAS Middle-Tier Administration Guide does a great job of defining when redeployment and rebuild of web applications might be necessary (see Appendix for links).

You must rebuild a web application if you, for example, made changes to the configuration, such as Java security, custom themes are created, after installing hotfixes that updated your web applications, and more.

Once you rebuild a web application, you must redeploy it.

Depending on your SAS environment, you typically have more than one SAS Web Application Server instance (for example, SASServer1_1 and SASServer2_1). The names of the SAS Web Application Servers depend on the products you have installed. Using the instructions.html file, you can find out which SAS web applications are deployed to which SAS Web Application Server instance. See Figure 3.18 for an example.

Figure 3.18: Instructions.html file

Overview

1. Warnings and Notices
2. SAS Management Console
3. SAS Application Servers
4. SAS Spawners
5. SAS Web Infrastructure Platform Data Server
6. SAS Deployment Tester Server
7. Operating System Services Scheduling Server
8. SAS Visual Analytics
9. SAS Information Retrieval Studio
10. SAS Web Infrastructure Platform Scheduling Services
11. Remote Services
12. SAS Environment Manager Configuration
13. SAS Environment Manager Agent Configuration
14. SAS Environment Manager Enablement Kit Server
15. SAS Web Server Configuration
16. Web Application Server
17. SAS Web Applications
18. Web Application Custom Content
19. Obtaining Additional Information

Configuring SAS Web Application Server Instance(s)

Host machine	l10b787.na.sas.com
Port	8080, 8443
Server Name	SASServer1
Configuration directory	C:\SAS\Config\Lev1\Web\WebAppServer\SASServer1_1
Log directory	C:\SAS\Config\Lev1\Web\WebAppServer\SASServer1_1\logs
	• SASWebInfrastructurePlatformServices9.4 • SASWebInfrastructurePlatformApplications9.4 • SASWIPAdmin9.4 • SASWIPResources9.4 • SASStoredProcess9.4

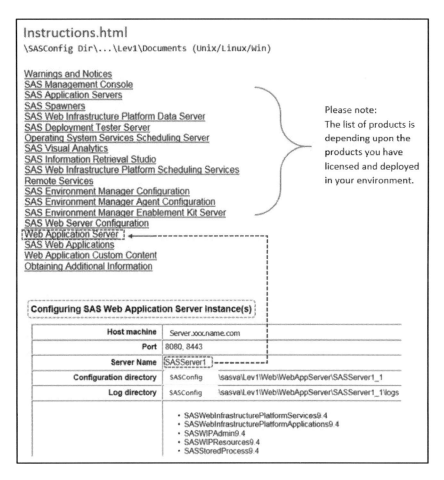

If you run into any problems during this process – or generally experience issues with the middle tier, the following SAS note will help you locate the log files to troubleshoot. See Usage Note 55426: Locating the log files for the SAS® 9.4 middle tier at: http://support.sas.com/kb/55/426.html

Remove Existing Configuration

This option enables you to completely remove some or all product configurations. Please note that removing a product configuration does not remove or uninstall the products itself.

Removing an existing configuration is not trivial because products and SAS services are dependent upon each other – and this is where it gets tricky: If you remove the configuration of a product that another product depends on, the dependent product would will not function anymore. So not only do you have to consider the actual configuration of a product, but also dependent configurations. If you remove configurations in the wrong way, worst case scenario would be that your SAS environment won't might not function anymore.

To be on the safe side, please check with SAS Technical Support before removing any configurations and, most importantly, run a backup before any changes are made. Please take a close look at Chapter 7, which is all about backing up and restoring in SAS.

Renew SAS Software and Update SID File in Metadata

Your SAS software is licensed on a periodic basis, usually for one year. After a certain period is reached, you must renew your SAS license to continue to use your SAS products. SAS is nice and doesn't just stop working; it warns you way before your software really stops. Unfortunately, experience has shown that, often, admins don't take those warnings seriously, with the result that – suddenly – no one can work anymore., which will end up in panic calls to SAS to get a new license. Another issue I see quite often is that SAS admins are not well informed about the entire renewal situation. So, let's take a closer look at it.

There are two licenses that you must consider: One, for your SAS Foundation and one for metadata. To renew the license file for your installed SAS Foundation software, you choose the **Renew SAS Software** option. To select a license file for metadata, choose **Update SID File in Metadata.**

Need-to-knows

Here are some important points to consider:

- SAS uses a file called SAS Installation Data (SID).
- The SAS Foundation license is renewed via Deployment Manager, **Renew SAS Software**.
- Products that rely on the middle tier require an update in metadata, using **Update SID File in Metadata**.
- Look at the SAS solutions that require an **Update SID File in Metadata**, listed in the following SAS Note:
  Usage Note 49750: To extend the expiration date for particular SAS® solutions and products, you must perform the "Update SID File in Metadata" task at
  http://support.sas.com/kb/49/750.html
- The SID file expires 90 days after the actual expiration date.
- Before these 90 days, you have a 45-day Grace period and a 45-day Warning period. The following. warning message will appear in your log file:
  WARNING:
  Your system is scheduled to expire on   (date)   , which is _(# of)_ days from now. Please contact your SAS Software Representative to obtain your updated setinit information. The SAS System will no longer function on or after that date.

To find out when your SID file expires, you can run the following SAS code:

```
proc setinit;
run;
```

The PROC SETINIT will show information about your license' *Warning* and *Grace* period.

Running the proc setinit in my environment, displays the following information:

```
Expiration:    14DEC2018.
Grace Period:  45 days (ending 28JAN2019).
Warning Period: 55 days (ending 24MAR2019).
```

In my example, the *Warning Period* ends on March 24, 2019, which means, on March 24 your SAS software will drop dead, or, more professionally speaking, will stop functioning. You probably might be asking yourself how the license expires after 90 days, yet my proc setinit output shows a Grace period of **45** days and a warning period of **55** days, which clearly sums up to **100** days.

> **Note:** The 90-day expiration period includes holidays or weekends. However, there is a logic built in to add extra days should the 90th day fall on a US weekend or holiday. The week SAS is closed for the winter break is considered as well, which explains why you might see different and additional numbers in your proc setinit output.
>
> Please note: this calculation is based on US contracts definition. Other countries might be calculated differently as holidays are different in each country.

I am going into all these details because this is a question that arises quite often, and I can see why. However, please do not start counting days but rather dig into the documentation and speak to your finance team to renew your license.

If you want to view the metadata setinit information, you can do so in SAS Management Console. This is available with SAS 9.4 Maintenance release 2 (M2). Figure 3.19 shows how to view the metadata setinit details.

Figure 3.19: View Metadata Setinit

You won't see any information if none of the solutions and products described in Usage Note 49750 are licensed: http://support.sas.com/kb/49/750.html

If an error such as …

```
A problem was encountered while renewing:
Apply SAS Foundation license file for renewal
For more information please see the log file: C:\Program
Files\SASHome\SASFoundation\9.4\setinit.log
Would you like to retry this installation?
```

occurs, the renewal process for SAS® 9.4 fails when applying the SAS® Foundation license file and returns a Renewal Failure error and references setinit.log might help: http://support.sas.com/kb/61/057.html.

Other errors that you might encounter:

Error:

```
A lock is not available for sashelp.core.catalog.
```

Solution:

Problem Note 56754: The SAS® Renewal Utility for SAS® software fails and the setinit.log file contains "ERROR: A lock is not available for SASHELP.CORE.CATALOG" at:http://support.sas.com/kb/56/754.html

Error:

```
A lock is not available for SASHELP.CORE.CATALOG, lock held by another
process
```

Solution:

Problem Note 52302: An error message indicates that your SAS® software license has expired and a subsequent message says that your core.sas7bcat file is locked at: http://support.sas.com/kb/52/302.html

License Help

The License Assistance page at https://support.sas.com/en/technical-support/license-assistance.html will help you find your information about Installation Reps and SAS Reps.

Should you ever be in a pickle and need a temporary license file, you can request it at:

Temporary License File, located at: https://login.sas.com/opensso/UI/Login?realm=/extweb&goto=https%3A%2F%2Fsupport.sas .com%2Fsastools%2Flerequest It requires you to have a SAS profile. Creating a profile is a piece of cake and the temporary license file site will provide the information. However, I would like to mention that using temporary setinit files each year as a "pass" for not paying attention to the warnings in the log files, is not a good practice – not at all! We might cotton on to you.

> **Tip:** Save the information about how to renew a license file, who to contact if one is needed, information about grace period and warning period and other information that is helpful when it comes to updating a license file, on a shared network location that is accessible by all admins. Consider that other admins or other personas might need to know about the licensing as well. If you store it on your local machine, no one else will be able to access that information.

Difference between SAS Installation Data and a SETINIT

SAS Installation Data (SID) includes customized installation information and customized product authorization information for your site. The setinit (the product authorization data) does the licensing work that enables SAS to run until your license expires. The SAS Installation Data (SID) includes your SETINIT. Take a look at Usage Note 23227: What is the difference between SAS Installation Data and a SETINIT? at http://support.sas.com/kb/23/227.html for more information.

We do not cover SAS installation in this book, however, if you are interested in learning about it, check out the SAS® Deployment Wizard and SAS® Deployment Manager 9.4: User's Guide at http://support.sas.com/documentation/installcenter/en/ikdeploywizug/66034/PDF/default/user .pdf

Manage SAS File Types

Choose this option on Windows to manage the products associated with file types. This option is only available if you have products installed that use file type associations, such as SAS Enterprise Guide for example. Figure 3.20 will provide you with an overview of the supported SAS file types. In the left column you can see file extensions that are associated with a SAS product.

Figure 3.20: Default Product for SAS File Types

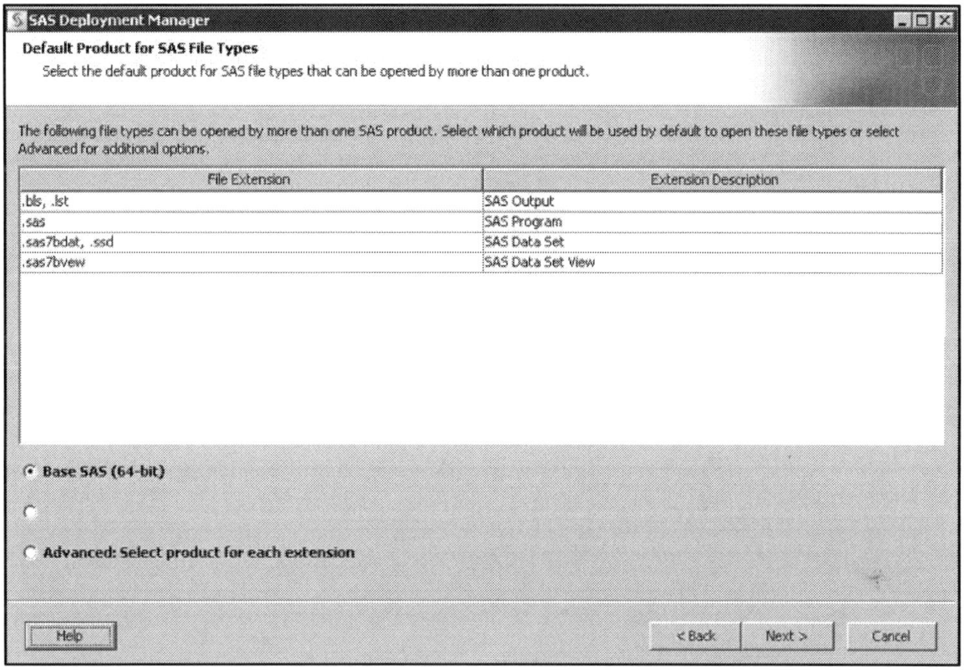

Update Host Name Reference

Use this feature to update any references to server names or a network domain name in your SAS environment. Here is how to update a host name reference:

- Run *Update Hostname Reference* with the user ID that installed the SAS software, or any administrator user ID that has full permissions on the OS.

- After the changes have been made, SAS will create a report for you showing the changes made. If follow up steps are necessary, you will be provided with instructions as well.

- When you run the tool, you can specify more than one machine name that is to be updated as shown in Figure 3.21.

Figure 3.21: Multiple Host Names

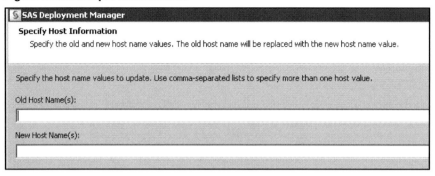

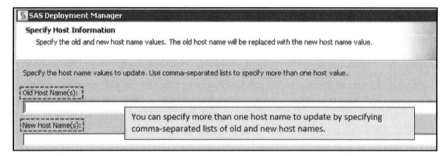

- You do not have to worry about specifying a wrong machine name. If SAS cannot find the machine name, you will receive a warning message.

Potential scenarios when you might use this tool are:

- Machine name has changed in a single-machine deployment or a single-machine deployment has been cloned to another machine.
- Multiple-machine deployment has been cloned to a new set of machines
- Metadata server has been cloned to a new machine
- Name of a SAS Application Server host machine has changed
- Network domain name has changed

Before we take a closer look at each scenario, I want to make sure you understand the details and consequences of using the Update Hostname Reference. To start out with, you need to understand that some SAS configuration files and metadata objects store machine names. To give you an example:

metaparms.sas in **\config_dir\Lev1\SASMeta\MetadataServer** includes the following information (snippet):

options metaserver="machine_name"

metaport=8561

The file *meta.parms* is used by the SAS backup process. If the machine name is wrong, the backup would fail. This is just an example to demonstrate how important machine names stored in SAS config files are. If you make changes in your SAS environment without using the Update Hostname Reference, parts of your environment might not work anymore.

Now let's look at each scenario in a little more detail.

Machine name has changed in a single-machine deployment or Single-machine deployment has been cloned to another machine

A machine name might change when you want to move your environment to another machine with a different host name, and in cases where you want to set up a failover/stand-by in case something happens. Creating a failover environment is not easy and requires careful considerations.

Multiple-machine deployment has been cloned to a new set of machines

Cloning a multi-machine SAS environment to a new set of machines is more challenging, because your SAS tiers are spread amongst several machines. When you clone a 3-machine environment, the environment to which you are cloning must have the same number of machines, the same topology, including the products installed and configured on each machine. Consider this carefully. Maybe it would be better for your case to do a new deployment and then use the Promotion tools to move content from the old machine to the new one. With this, you also have to consider that Promotion is used for moving partial content, not the entire content of an environment at once. You can use Promotion for your SAS folders and its contents. Before you clone an environment, I would recommend contacting SAS to discuss, simply to make sure that you have all the information needed to make an educated decision.

> **Note:** When you clone SAS environments for failover purposes, you must be sure to keep the failover machine up-to-date. This means, every hot fix, every patch etc. has to be installed on both machines. If you upgrade a maintenance release on one, you must upgrade the other environment as well.

Metadata server has been cloned to a new machine

Remember when we talked about the different tiers in the SAS Architecture chapter? Suppose you run all SAS tiers on a single machine. Now, at one point, you want to "source out" the metadata server on its own machine. In such a case, you would clone the metadata server only.

Name of a SAS Application Server host machine has changed

This option can be used in scenarios where your SAS Metadata Server, the SAS Application Servers ,and the SAS middle tier all run on different machines. If the machine name of the SAS Application Servers changes, the metadata server tier and middle tier would remain untouched.

Network domain name has changed

If your SAS environment is installed in a network domain and the name of this domain changes, you must use this option to make sure that all domain name occurrences in your environment will be changed

> **Note:** Please pay close attention to the DNS lookup selection that you make (selected/not selected) as it affects how information for your environments' configuration files are updated – or not. The DNS lookup identifies all forms of the host names that must actually be updated. The instructions will let you know when to select it and when not, but I want to explicitly mention it as because it can cause your environment not to function anymore.

Best Practice

It is a best practice to not use IP addresses but hostnames. It is easier to maintain. Also, to be on the safe side, once you ran the Update Hostname Reference, run a scan afterward to see whether there are any leftover places with the old machine names.

Failover

If you are setting up a failover environment, please take a look Do You Have a Disaster Recovery Plan for Your SAS® Infrastructure? at:

https://support.sas.com/resources/papers/proceedings17/SAS0565-2017.pdf. It provides you with great details.

Log Files

In case you are experiencing any problems, you can look at the log files to look for any errors and / or warnings. The log files are stored here:

```
SAS-configuration-directory/Levn/Logs/Configure
```

The name of the log files:

```
software-component_changeHost_date-and-time.log
```

If you are experiencing any problems with the SAS Deployment Manager tool, you can look at the log files here:

- On Windows Vista, Windows 7, and Windows 2008:
  C:\Users*user*\AppData\Local\SAS\SASDeploymentWizard\9.4\sdm.log

- On other Windows systems:
  C:\Documents and Settings*user*\Local Settings\Application Data\SAS\SASDeploymentWizard\9.4\sdm.log

- On UNIX systems:
  user's-home-directory/.SASAppData/SASDeploymentWizard/9.4/sdm.log

Best Practice: Before using the Deployment Manager's Update Host Reference, you **must** run a backup. Please see the backup Chapter 7 for detailed information about backups. This is because changing a machine name or domain name is a rather serious task, so it might not be a bad idea to check with SAS Technical Support to discuss your scenario before making any changes. Any questions or requests that go beyond the scope of SAS Technical Support will be referred to the appropriate person or team who can discuss this with you. Also, changing host names is not something that you should do on the fly, let alone during a time where user traffic is the busiest. Consider to setting up an appropriate time window when such a change could be done.

Apply Hot Fixes

Hot fixes are important. They fix critical and reoccurring problems. They are important for your SAS environment's maintenance and well-being. If a defect in the SAS software has been detected and has a major effect on the usage or operation of SAS, alerts or high priority hot fixes are created. Typically, hot fixes that have been created in one maintenance release are included in the next maintenance release.

Best Practice: You do not have to jump on every hot fix that is being released, as applying a hot fix is a very case-by-case situation. A hot fix might not apply to your SAS environment or to your SAS products, so there is no need to install it.

A best practice when to install hot fixes is:
- If it is applicable to your environment
- If you want that specific hot fix because of a feature you want to have
- If SAS Technical Support tells you to

Installing a Hot Fix

You know the saying "RTFM"? Well, there is no better place to use it. It is so important to read the instructions for each hot fix because the ways to install different hotfixes are never the same. So, the argument "I did it once and know how it works" doesn't fly here.

Staying up-to-date on Hot Fixes

To stay up-to-date on hot fixes, check out the SAS Communities for alerts and tips.

Hot Fix Analyze Tool

SAS provides you with a tool that allows you to analyze your environment and that provides you with a report about eligible hot fixes. The tool is called SAS Hot Fix Analysis, Download and Deployment Tool (SASHFADD), and can be downloaded from the support website here: http://ftp.sas.com/techsup/download/hotfix/HF2/SASHFADD.html

There are fixes that are not supported by the SASHFADD tool; see Usage Note 52718: SAS Hot Fixes and Patches not supported by SASHFADD, see http://support.sas.com/kb/52/718.html

Update Existing Configuration

When you upgrade software (maintenance release) or add new products, you run the install with the SAS Deployment Wizard. Check out the resources in the Appendix.

Another scenario where you might use this option is when you must configure an already updated or upgraded SAS product.

Change Passphrase

When we talk about passphrases, we also need to talk about encryption. Let's first start with how SAS handles encryption. SAS encrypts data at rest with the goal to protect the passwords in your SAS configuration files, metadata and data sets. You can also encrypt passwords in transit.

A passphrase is similar to a password in that it can be used as an addition to encryption for passwords that are stored in metadata. If you do not use passphrases, the metadata server uses a basic encryption, which is SASPROPRIATERY, a 32-bit key. Using a passphrase makes for stronger encryption; a passphrase is an encryption key that is stronger and more secure than a fixed key. You must be an unrestricted user in order to make any such changes to the passphrase.

Your stored passwords can be protected with encryption keys available with SAS. Your passwords are stored with this encryption type. With a passphrase, you can update the format that is used for your stored passwords.

> **Note:** When you introduce, change, or clear a passphrase, all passwords in login objects within the specified metadata server are affected. Make sure you have a current backup before you set a passphrase.

Locale Setup manager

The locale setup comes into play with National Language Support (NLS). For example, you can switch from en_US to UTF8 in order to support a much wider range of language characters, which is helpful for example, if you are working in a global environment. (such as US and Germany).

Should you run into a problem concerning the *Locale Setup Manager*, check out the SAS Note to see whether it applies, see Problem Note 60663: SAS® Locale Setup Manager might not change the locale value for SAS® Foundation if the SAS® default encoding is Unicode at: http://support.sas.com/kb/60/663.html

Uninstalling SAS Software

The SAS Deployment Manager is used to uninstall the entire SAS environment or only certain products that are installed in the SASHOME directory (see chapter 2, SAS Architecture, for more information about SASHOME). You can uninstall SAS software without using the SAS Deployment Wizard by doing a quiet uninstall via command line. Before you uninstall any products, please be sure to run a backup. It's important to not only run the metadata server backup, but to run your file system backup as well!

There are a few things that you have to consider when uninstalling using the SAS Deployment Wizard and uninstalling using the command line.

Once you uninstall your SAS software, please make sure that every single file and folder are in fact gone. Should the software not have been removed entirely, please see Installation Note 37352: The procedure for completely uninstalling SAS software from a Windows operating environment at http://support.sas.com/kb/37/352.html (this SAS Note provides information for prior SAS versions as well. Please just focus on SAS 9.4).

Video: Uninstalling SAS on Windows, at: https://www.youtube.com/watch?v=4s3cQOg0As0

If you run SAS 9.4 M1, M2, the following SAS Note might be helpful in case you run into the following problem: When you use SAS® Deployment Manager 9.4 to uninstall software, the process stops and the summary of uninstalled products is blank: http://support.sas.com/kb/57/406.html

If you do run M1 or M2, this is the documentation for upgrading a maintenance release, which you will need when you upgrade to the newest maintenance release tomorrow! http://support.sas.com/software/updates/index.html

> **Important:** Before you uninstall any products, please be sure to run a backup. It's important to not only run the metadata server backup, but to run your file system backup as well!

The Deployment Manager offers additional tasks which will not be discussed in this book.

SAS Web Administration Console

The SAS Web Administration Console comes into play for the SAS middle tier. You can use this tool to monitor who is currently logged on to your SAS web applications (such as SAS Studio or even SAS Environment Manager. etc.); another helpful task that is provided is the ability to report on users' log on and log off activities and failed logons, and the option to force a logoff. There are many more features available.

Some of the information that you monitor in the SAS Web Administration Console can also be monitored using SAS Environment Manager. Once in a while, admins ask what which they should use: the web admin console or SAS Environment Manage? You can't really compare the two as because they are each fulfilling different purposes. A few types of information can be monitored in both applications. As you can see, SAS Management

Console, SAS Environment Manager and SAS Web Administration Console might share a few functionalities, but in the great scheme of things, they are SAS admin tools each fulfilling a different purpose. All SAS admin tools "intermingle" somehow at some point, but you cannot choose one to administer everything. You can access the SAS Web Administration Console, using an admin account that is member of the SAS Administrators group, with the following url: `http(s)://server:port/SASAdmin`

The server and port are the host name and port number of your web application server.

Once you have logged on successfully, and voila! You'll see the console as shown as Figure 3.22. Depending on the SAS products you have licensed, you might see different or additional functionalities listed.

Figure 3.22: SAS Web Administration Console

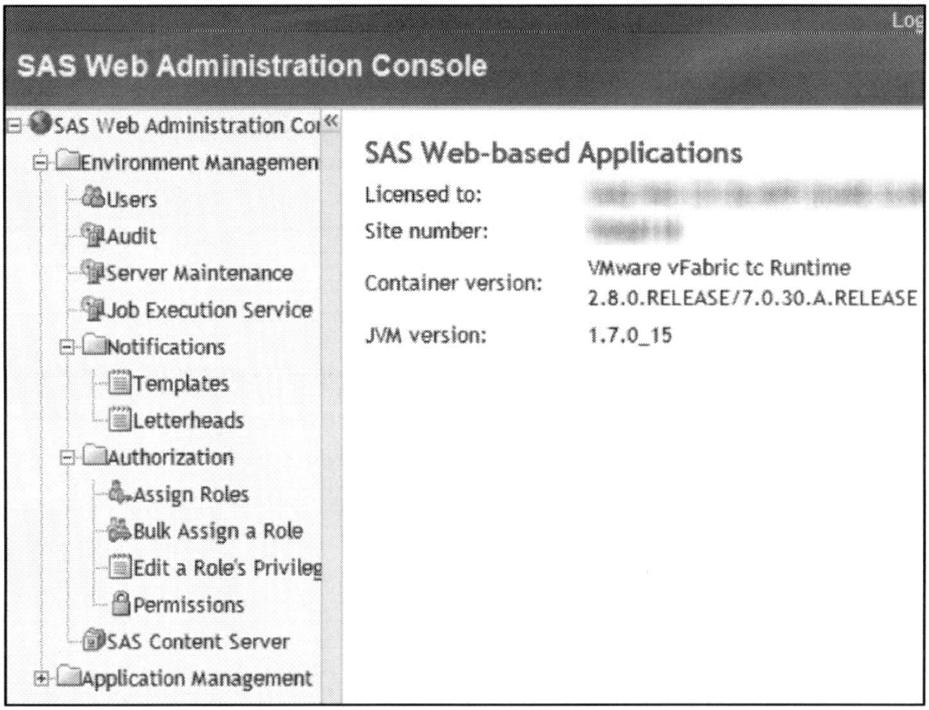

> **Note:** Depending on the SAS products you have licensed, you might see different or additional functionalities listed.

If you look at, Figure 3.22 you will see a *SAS Content Server* entry on the left.

So, to make things even more confusing, I would like to throw in the *SAS Content Server Administration Console.* It's a mouthful. Your SAS Content Server is a content repository that stores content such as documents, reports, and images that are created by your users using SAS web clients. Your Content Server starts automatically when the web application server is started.

If you click on the SAS Content Server in the SAS Web Administration Console, you see the content that is stored in the SAS Content Server repository. Folders for this content (create, rename etc.), or permissions on who can write to or see or modify these folders, are managed in the SAS Content Server Administration Console.

Summary

This concludes the introduction to the SAS Administration Tools. I hope that the basics, documentations, tips and notes are helpful to get you started with your SAS admin tools. As mentioned earlier, even though the administration consoles and its features intermingle at times, they are nonetheless used for distinctive tasks. Knowing how all the admin tools work are a great start for getting ready to tackle the administration beast.

I would like to end this chapter with a quote – the author is unknown, but I bet you everything they are an admin: "*In case you forgot to remind yourself this morning: Your butt is perfect. Your smile lights up the room. Your mind is insanely cool. You are way more than enough. And you are doing an amazing job at life.*" Replace "at life" with "at SAS Administration!"

Chapter 4: Do I Know You? A Quick Review on Users, Groups, and Roles in SAS 9.4

Introduction to User, Group and Role Management

In this chapter, I would like to talk about users, groups and roles in SAS. The SAS documentation gives a good introduction on how to create users, groups and roles, so let's talk a bit about what users, groups and roles in SAS are and how they work. Understanding the user, group and role management is important when it comes to building your SAS environment.

Let's start by leaving SAS for a moment and just think about users and groups from an authentication (domain) perspective in general. Users and groups can be created either

- On a local machine, or/and
- On a computer network using directory service accounts such as LDAP or Active Directory

You create users and groups to "open the doors" for your users: they can log on to your system, run code, access data that you store in system folders, etc.

Now let's turn to SAS and talk specifically about users and groups in SAS. In SAS, you create users and groups in metadata, using SAS Management Console or SAS Environment Manager. By creating users and groups in metadata, you, too, open the door for users, just this time the door for the SAS metadata world.

> **Note:** You can use SAS clients, such as SAS Enterprise Guide, SAS Studio, etc., *without* creating users in SAS. Your users just simply use their OS credentials.

However, to use all the features in SAS 9.4, especially security, and to use reporting tools such as SAS Environment Manager, you must have users in SAS metadata. As a best practice, SAS recommends creating and maintaining your users and groups in metadata.

Aside from users and groups, as mentioned in the title of this chapter, there are also roles. Before we will dive deeper into talking more about users and groups, let's check off the roles.

Roles

As an example of a role in a different context: User Gwendolyn has an access card to enter a building, but her access card doesn't give her the capability to go on the floor where the finance department is located. Benji is a manager, so his access card provides the capability to access every floor and every department in that building. If we take that example and apply it to SAS, Gwendolyn might have the capability to use certain features in a SAS client, whereas user Benji might have the capability of using all features of a SAS client. Even SAS administrators can have different capabilities, which comes in handy for a team of admins, where each admin fulfills a different *role*.

To give you an example, let's look at some of the admin roles in SAS and the different capabilities that they provide:

Figure 4.1: Admin Roles

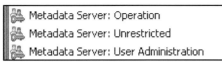

Metadata Server: Operation. Admins can create custom and project repositories and operate the metadata server (start, stop, pause, resume, quiesce), using the Server Manager plug-in in SAS Management Console.

Metadata Server: Unrestricted. Admins with this role applied have all capabilities and full access to metadata. However, they cannot read users' passwords.

Metadata Server: User Administration.
 Admins can create and manage non-admin users, groups and roles, internal accounts, logins and authentication domains

Important key points about metadata-based application roles

- Roles do not protect data or metadata. This is an important point and often misunderstood. Roles just control which features in a particular application are available to which users.

- An application feature that is under role-based management is called a capability. Each role provides multiple capabilities. A user or group can be in multiple roles, such as access to Server Manager, access to certain functions in SAS Enterprise Guide, etc.

- Not all applications have roles. Not all application features are under role management. Each application that supports roles provides a fixed set of capabilities. You cannot convert a feature that is not a capability into a capability. If you have the need to apply capabilities that are not part of a role, it is a best practice (a very strong recommended best practice), to create new custom roles and apply the capabilities you need to this new role. If you use an already existing role, it defeats the purpose, as every already existing role fulfills a certain purpose. If you modify it, you change the roles' role that it plays in the SAS environment. Remember it that way: every role has a role to play, each of which is different. In a cast of a play you won't find one and the same characters twice on stage, if that makes sense.

> **Note**: Custom Tasks in SAS Enterprise Guide:
> You have the option to register custom tasks as capabilities in SAS Enterprise Guide. Generally, you can allow or disallow custom tasks. If you allow them, you can restrict these custom tasks to just approved tasks. The following blog is a great resource:

Controlling access to custom tasks in SAS Enterprise Guide at https://blogs.sas.com/content/sasdummy/2013/01/07/controlling-access-to-custom-tasks-in-sas-enterprise-guide/

- Capabilities are additive. There are no negative capabilities (capabilities that limit what a user can do). It is not possible to deny a capability (capabilities are either granted or not granted).

- Capabilities can be categorized as follows:

  ○ explicit capabilities
    Can be incrementally added to or removed from any role (other than the unrestricted role, which always provides all explicit capabilities). Most roles have explicit capabilities.

  ○ implicit capabilities
    are permanently bound to a certain role. The metadata server's roles provide implicit capabilities. For example, the user administration role provides the capability to add users, but there is no explicit *Create Users* capability.

  ○ contributed capabilities
    are implicit or explicit capabilities that are assigned through role aggregation. If you designate one role as a contributing role for another role, all of the first role's capabilities become contributed capabilities for the second role.

- Important: You cannot assign permissions to a role. You cannot assign capabilities to a group.
  A user cannot temporarily assume or relinquish a role. All of a user's roles are active at all times.

For more resources about roles can be found in the Appendix.

OK, now we can check off the roles. Next, lets dive into the world of users and groups in SAS.

Users

Let's get back to users and groups. The SAS Management Console: Guide to Users and Permissions explains it in the following way:

In order to make access distinctions and track user activity, security systems must know who is making each request.

This goes back to what I mentioned earlier, that you have to have users in metadata in order to apply metadata security, in order to do reporting, auditing and monitoring using SAS Environment Manager, etc.

So, the main purpose of user administration is to provide information that helps SAS make this determination. The central piece of user information that the SAS environment requires is **one external account ID for each user**. The SAS environment uses its copy of these IDs to establish a unique SAS identity for each connecting user. All of a user's group memberships, role memberships, and permission assignments are ultimately tied to their SAS identity.

If you do not want to create your users in metadata interactively by using the User Manager plugin in SAS Management Console, you can write a program that performs these tasks as batch processes. You can do this using the user import macros. A link to the documentation is in the Appendix.

> **Note:**
> For identification purposes, only the account IDs are needed. SAS does not maintain copies of external passwords for identification purposes.
>
> Leaving the official doc, let me continue in the Anja-style. For the OS users and SAS users, see Figure 4.2.

Figure 4.2: A visual depiction of OS users and SAS users

Operating System/LDAP/AD   **SAS Metadata Server**

OS/LDAP/AD/Database accounts are on the left in the oval figure. And SAS accounts are on the right.

Example

If we create a user in SAS metadata using SAS Management Console's or SAS Environment Manager's User Manager plug-in, that is associated with an external user ID, it could look like Figure 4.3.

Figure 4.3: A visual depiction of OS user Ben and SAS user Benji

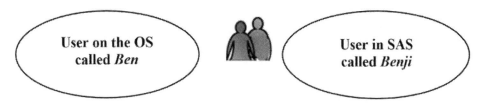

SAS user Benji uses OS user Ben in the background, meaning, user Benji is associated with user Ben.

In a more professional manner, this is the official description of a SAS user definition (aka login):

A login is a SAS copy of information about an external account. Every login must include a user ID. In a login for a Windows account, the ID must be qualified (for example, user@company.com), domain\user, or machine\user.

So, in our case, using **Ben** as the OS account and **Benji** as the SAS account, the SAS user ID in SAS Management Console or SAS Environment Manager, *User Manager plug-in*, would look like Figure 4.4.

Figure 4.4: Metadata and OS user

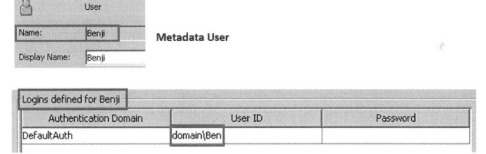

The explanation above is important when it comes to authentication. When a user logs on to a SAS client, such as SAS Enterprise Guide, the SAS user ID is verified in the background to make sure the users are who they say they are.

> **Note:** You must log on as an admin user to be able to work with user IDs. You can either use the unrestricted user ID sasadm@saspw or an admin user that has the capability to manage users. This capability is given with a role. An example for a role that provides this capability is *Metadata Server: User Administration*

So, going back to users, SAS identities, OS accounts and authentication, Figure 4.5 shows nicely how it works.

Figure 4.5: Host Authentication.

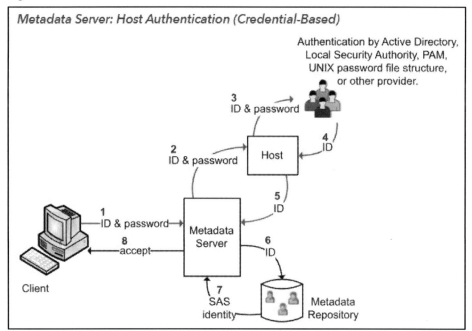

When a user launches a SAS client, an authentication process with two phases occurs:

In the verification phase, the system ensures that the user is who he or she claims to be. An example for a credential-based host authentication is as follows:

- The client prompts the user for an ID and password.
- The user enters credentials that are known to the metadata server's **host**.
- The client sends the credentials to the metadata server.
- The metadata server passes the credentials to its host for authentication.
- If the host determines that the user has a valid account, the host returns the authenticated user ID to the metadata server.

In the SAS identity phase, the system resolves the authenticated user ID to a particular SAS identity. In this phase, SAS examines its copies of user IDs in metadata in an attempt to find one that matches the authenticated user ID. Simply put: Once the user is authenticated by the operating system, the metadata server goes through the users in the User Manager and checks whether there is a metadata identity that has the successfully authenticated user login with the matching metadata user ID.

 If a matching user ID is found, a connection is established under the owning identity. The owning identity is the user or group whose definition includes an operating system login with the matching metadata user ID.

If we throw an additional authentication provider in the mix, such as LDAP, the following Figure 4.6 shows a comparison of authentication.

Figure 4.6: Metadata Server

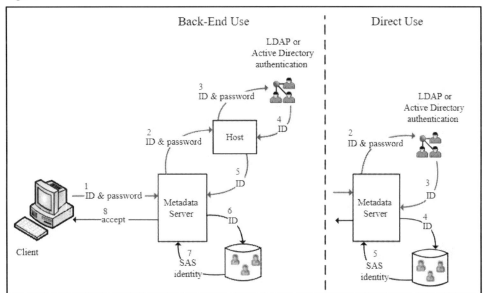

More information about the link to the different authentication mechanisms can be found in the Appendix.

What if the metadata server cannot find a matching user in metadata (User Manager)?

When SAS is installed, two implicit groups are created by default for you: PUBLIC and SASUSERS. If the metadata server cannot find a metadata user in the User Manager that stores the successfully authenticated OS identity, the user is authenticated as a so called **public-only** user. Literally. A public user does not belong to a particular group and does not have a particular user ID and is therefore considered a general person without any metadata user affiliation.

So, lets dig deeper into our user and group adventure and let's talk about PUBLIC and SASUSERS.

As mentioned prior, when SAS is installed, two so called **implicit** groups are created by default for you: PUBLIC and SASUSERS.

PUBLIC and SASUSERS exist in every metadata server environment, no matter what products you have licensed.

SASUSERS includes all successfully authenticated OS users that are tied to a metadata user ID. A user successfully outside-of-SAS-authenticated with a metadata identity (a user that you see in the User Manager) makes a user member of the SASUSERS group.

So, if you have the scenario:

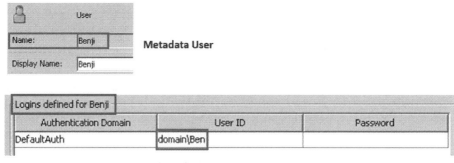

User Benji is initially identified as a member of SASUSERS.

If you don't have the above, if you don't see a user ID for that user in metadata, the user is authenticated as PUBLIC. Just keep this rule in mind whenever you work with users and groups:

A user successfully-outside-of-SAS-authenticated with a metadata identity (a user that you see in the User Manager) makes a user member of the SASUSERS group.

A user successfully-outside-of-SAS-authenticated without a metadata identity (user is not in the User Manager) makes a user a member of the PUBLIC group.

Now, knowing this, think about it in terms of security: Would you want to let just everyone into your house or only people that you know? It's the same concept. I don't want users that are not known to the metadata server messing with my metadata. I want to control who accesses my assets, and for that reason, I make sure that PUBLIC users will never be able to get into my environment. Just keep this in mind for now. You will need this when we talk about security later on.

Note: There are always exceptions to the rule, and it might be useful in your case to allow public access. The general rule is to avoid it. This would have to be decided case by case and should be very well thought through.

At this point, you might be asking yourself: If users that are created in metadata and are associated with a successfully authenticated OS user ID, why are they put into a "non-explicit-metadata-user" group called SASUSERS? And, if SASUSERS means there is a metadata identity, wouldn't that make it explicit?

These are great questions. To address these questions, we move on to groups in SAS.

Groups in SAS (SAS User Groups)

To recap, we identified users in the User Manager that are associated with an OS account as members of an implicit group called SASUSERS. Let's assume you have 500 individual users. Would you want to assign permissions on objects 500 times – for each individual user? Or, would you rather minimize the effort and use groups to assign permissions to objects? I would definitely choose the latter!

Let me give you a good group example:

I am working in a department that is called *Customer Success*. The department consists of two different teams:

We have a team of :

1. *Systems Engineers* – handling all things technical (I am a member of this team)
2. *Customer Success Managers* – who focus on post-sales activities.

Rather than giving permissions to each individual Customer Success team employee, the employees have been put into **groups**. All groups in our department are: A group for System Engineers, a group for Customer Success Managers, a group for managers, and groups for each business unit the Customer Success Managers work in.

So, you can see, all employees have been placed into groups based on:

- job description and tasks, the type of work
- data we each need to access, and
- responsibilities, etc.

Data and information our managers access might not be accessible to us employees; technical info for Systems Engineers might not be that important to Customer Success Managers, and so forth. To make things easier and distinct, these *explicit* groups have been created.
Yes, of course, you must create individual users first to be able to create groups, but the end goal for creating users in metadata is to minimize the administration and maintenance effort as much as possible by using groups.

Going back to the questions about why SASUSERS is being called an implicit group even though it seems to be explicit. Every user in your SAS environment is member of SASUSERS, and remains a member of SASUSERS, even if put into an explicit group. Going back to my previous Customer Success Department example, each individual member of the Customer Success department is a member of SASUSERS.

When I first started as an admin, many moons ago, I got dizzy with all the implicit and explicit, but it is really pretty simple if you think about it in terms of the example:

Benji is a Systems Engineer. When he logs on to SAS, he is authenticated as member of SASUSERS. But, on top of that, the metadata server is smart and realizes that there is another group for Benji, called Systems Engineers. And even so Benji remains in the SASUSERS group, the permissions that might be explicitly set for the custom group Benji is a member of, take precedence.

SASUSERS and PUBLIC will come into play when we talk about permissions later. For now, it is just important that you understand the concept of users, groups, roles, explicit and implicit groups.

Bottom line:

In summary, once you create individual users, you can then create groups and organize your users into groups. A user can belong to multiple groups; however, this must be carefully thought through. Interestingly, the question on whether to create users first or groups first, seems to kick of passionate discussions at times. To me, it fits into the "what was first, the chicken or the egg" category, and is a rather philosophical question each customer has to answer for themselves. If you are wondering whether to create users first or groups first, I think it is easier to bring all my users into my SAS environment and then create groups based on my users. Either way, the main ingredient for a successful user and group set up is to create a concept, a plan, beforehand. It does not make sense to come up with wild group names if they don't fulfill a purpose. I would not create a group called Dogs and add Cats to it.

The best advice I can give you:

Think about your user base. Are you responsible for one department, one team, or several? If the latter, does it make sense to create groups based on team names, did someone else before you maybe already create users? And further, do some users access the same data? Do users share data? What tasks do your users fulfill? What SAS clients are they using, what output are they creating, and so forth. These are examples for criteria that you should use before you put groups into place.

Whether you decide to create groups first or, users first, – what matters is that you have a good strategy in place.

Good-to-Know: What if I Already Have Users and Groups in LDAP or AD?

If you use LDAP or AD, SAS provides you with an option to import your LDAP/AD users and groups into SAS metadata (they will appear in the SAS Management Console's User Manager). Check out *Usage Note 40628: Automating the addition of users and groups to a SAS® Metadata Repository*, at: http://support.sas.com/kb/40/628.html (that's a short link to type, right?)

Let's summarize what we have covered so far about user, groups, and roles:

- It is a best practice to create users and groups in metadata using the User Manager plug-in in SAS Management Console or SAS Environment Manager, to synchronize users and groups with an enterprise directory like Active Directory or LDAP.

- Metadata user IDs are associated with operating system/LDAP/AD or database accounts.

- Metadata users are authenticated with the operating system before getting access to metadata.

- After successful authentication on the OS, users are considered members of the two implicit SAS groups PUBLIC and SASUSERS.

With that, we can check off the introduction to users, groups and roles in SAS 9.4. Well, almost, we have to address one more thing: **Internal SAS Accounts**.

So far, we were talking about external users that are associated with a SAS identity (SASUSERS)– hopefully – because if not, they are public. Now, for good reasons, SAS implemented another group of users called *internal* SAS users.

SAS Internal Accounts

As the name implies, these user IDs are not in any way associated with an external account but are only known to SAS internally. If you don't want to leave your house, you don't have to care about anything that is happening outside. No street rules, no guidelines, no rules, no structure to follow; because you decided to stay inside and follow your own internal rules – which makes them internal rules, so to speak. Same with SAS internal users. Internal accounts do not really care about external users, policies, etc. They are solely focused on what is going on inside SAS. Think of it as a SAS account seclusion.

Internal SAS users are only known to SAS and are therefore authenticated internally only. You'll recognize an internal user by the @-sign and the ending *saspw*. A good example is the unrestricted SAS admin account: **sasadm@saspw**. Because these accounts are internal and known only by SAS without any external "ties" or associations, they are easier to maintain. They are not affected by external password changes and there is minimal risk of security exposure.

Note: Even though internal user accounts are easier to maintain, <u>do not</u> create regular users as internal user. Only external users can establish SAS workspace server sessions, and those are needed if you want your users to use your SAS environment appropriately.

Another reason not to use internal accounts for general users is that users and groups should be subject to restrictions and rules that you put into place, including providing credentials for access. You want to know who does what, and what to monitor and report, Internal accounts should be used for SAS internal purposes only.

The following are some internal users that SAS needs and creates per by default:

sasadm@saspw

This is an unrestricted user, who can see and do everything in metadata. The unrestricted admin user is not subjected to permissions. It's the Superhero account amongst the admins.

sastrust@saspw

This is the SAS Trusted user, also known as the impersonator amongst the internal accounts. Instead of getting my newspaper on Saturday mornings, my dog gets it for me. I trust my dog Jasper that she will not shred, roll and then eat my newspaper, but bring it to me safely. I trust her and therefore she fulfills the "getting the newspaper tasks" for me. In other words, my dog acts as **sastrust**. It is something that doesn't affect or interest the outside world and is something that is internal to the Fischers' only.

sasevs@saspw

That is the account the SAS Environment Manager Server and its SAS Environment Manager Agents use to communicate with each other. The sasevs@saspw account could be compared with a video connection between two parties. I (SAS Env Manager Agent) Skype with my parents, Eri and Harald (Env Manager Servers), every Sunday (predictable). They are in Germany, I am in Cary, North Carolina, in the United States. The internet connection (sasevs@saspw) works well most of the time, which means, our communication and exchange of information works well. On some days, however, the connection is bad, and our information exchange is interrupted. You could say sasevs@saspw has the hiccups. When this hiccup happens between SAS Environment Manager Server and the SAS Environment Manager Agents, it means you would not get any information about your resources or any reports in the SAS Environment Manager tool.

webanon@saspw

This is an internal anonymous web account that you can use to give web clients access to your web services without them having to put in credentials. By using webanon you are opening it all up a bit; using the webanon user, the clients get access through this user. The webanon@saspw account could probably be compared to a *grandpa-said-its-ok-but-maybe-mom-said-no-but-I-cannot-remember* situation.

For documentation reference, see Appendix.

Why Internal Accounts?

Being internal and known by SAS only without any "ties" or associations externally makes it nice and easy to maintain. Internal accounts don't care about external password changes for example. Another great advantage is that you do not have to create dedicated external OS accounts for processes that might be purely internal to SAS.

I hope that the SAS Users, Groups and Roles excursion is helpful to you as you go along with setting up, administering and maintaining your SAS environment. It is much needed knowledge for putting a good security structure into place and for understand who does what in your environment.

Before we conclude, we have to go over one more thing, to make the user and group management discussion complete. We have to talk about *Authentication Domains*.

Authentication Domains

When talking about authentication domains, I am referring to the field shown in Figure 4.6.

Figure 4.6: Authentication Domain field

Logins defined for Benji		
Authentication Domain	User ID	Password
DefaultAuth	domain\Ben	

As you know now, users in SAS metadata are associated with an OS/LDAP/AD/Database account. Going back to the example with Benji, you see one OS account in the properties of the metadata for user ID Benji. What you also see is a field for Authentication Domain. In this case, it shows *DefaultAuth*. An Authentication Domain comes into play for outbound logins. Outbound means, a user who is already authenticated by the metadata server makes a request for a workspace server, or, wants to access an external database. Everything that goes outside the initial (inbound) metadata server authentication. Inbound logins disregard and do not care about authentication domains. The DefaultAuth is only used to determine the user's metadata identity.

What if my user Benji does not only have to access data on the operating system, but, has to access data in Oracle as well? The logical thing to do would be – based on what we have learned so far – to probably create a new user ID in metadata for user Benji. But this time, we won't use the OS account, but will use the database user ID and password. Close, but not quite:

The beautiful thing about the users in metadata is that one metadata user ID can be associated with different external identities. Let's look at an example for user Benji. In addition to the DefaultAuth user ID, Benji also needs access to Oracle data. And for that reason, I simply add Benji's user ID for Oracle in his metadata server user ID. Now my metadata user ID looks like that in Figure 4.7.

Figure 4.7: Additional Authentication Domain

Logins defined for Benji		
Authentication Domain	User ID	Password
DefaultAuth	domain\Ben	
OraAuth	BenOracle	

To make sure the metadata server understands what type of connection it must establish for this user, as soon as a user logs on with a user ID specified in the metadata ID, the metadata server looks for all logins in that user ID and checks if there is one that fits. For Benji, he accesses Oracle using the credentials BenOracle. The metadata server looks if there is such a user ID in Benji's metadata definition. Oracle is just one example. You can store database accounts, other OS accounts etc. in a user definition in metadata.

You could say: The reason why we use authentication domains is to simply allow separation of user IDs stored under one metadata identity. Think of an authentication domain as an address. If I visit my friends, I know exactly which direction I have to go. These directions could be called FriendAuth. If I go to work, I know how to get there – let's call it WorkAuth.

Authentication domains are used to even further qualify what user IDs are attached to a metadata server user.

> **Best Practice:** Whenever you create an authentication domain to qualify an additional external user ID, make sure you use names that make sense. Naming an Authentication domain for Oracle or any other databases something like ABCAuth doesn't help if another admin has to administer, or , if you need to make changes later on. It is also important for troubleshooting purposes.

There is a great discussion about Authentication Domains on the SAS Administration and Deployment Community, which might be helpful to you. Paul Homes from Metacoda explains authentication domains in a great way, thinking of them as a tagging mechanism, "they are used to tag which credentials/logins can be used with which servers."

Summary

Let's summarize what we covered in this chapter:

- It is a best practice to create users and groups in metadata using the User Manager plug-in in SAS Management Console or SAS Environment Manager.

- Metadata user IDs are associated with operating system/LDAP/AD or database accounts.

- Metadata users are authenticated with the operating system, or LDAP/AD or internal before getting access to metadata.

- After successful authentication on the OS, users are considered members of the two implicit SAS groups PUBLIC and SASUSERS, sometimes Public-only.

- Internal SAS accounts are used for internal SAS use, and internal use only.

- Authentication domains are used to further associated a metadata identity with external logins.

- Before you start creating groups, make sure you have a good plan in place. Think about the teams or departments users are in, what data they might have to access and so forth.

What else?

There is a good amount of documentation out there. My recommendation is: Do not drive yourself nuts by feeling that you must actually read each and every single article, page and book about Users, Groups and Roles management. In fact, I would like to recommend that – for now– you focus on nothing but users, groups, roles and authentication domains. Everything user ultimately ends in authentication and authorization. We will discuss SAS security in a little bit. If you do want to read up on users, groups, roles and authentication domains, see the Appendix for link references.

Chapter 5: Metadata Library Administration in SAS 9.4

Introduction

Working with many new SAS administrators, I realized that understanding how external data can be created and accessed from within SAS metadata, doesn't seem to be that easy. For that reason, I would like to start out by going away of how to create libraries in SAS metadata, and I would like to talk more generally about how to create libraries in SAS Foundation or SAS Enterprise Guide for a moment.

Libraries in Base SAS

SAS programmers access external data sources, such as data sets stored on the operating system, or database data, etc. to be able to run code, create projects, produce output, and so on. To make that data available, a programmer creates a so called *LIBNAME statement* that associates a SAS library with a physical location. An example LIBNAME statement is:

```
LIBNAME name "c:\sas\data";
```

A LIBNAME statement associates a name of a libref with a physical location.

LIBNAME is the SAS syntax, **name** is a placeholder for whatever name you would like to create, and **c:\sas\data** is the location where the data resides.

Once a LIBNAME statement has been submitted, you can then refer to the data in that location using that libref that you used in your LIBNAME statement. So, when you code, you reference the library to point to the location of the data set(s) that you want to access.

Let's walk through an example.
I am storing some of my data sets in **C:\SAS\data\Anja.**

For this example, I am using SAS Enterprise Guide, and am submitting the following code:

```
LIBNAME DEMO "c:\sas\data\Anja";
```

The result is shown in Figure 5.1.

Figure 5.1: Assigning a LIBNAME statement

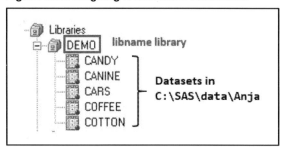

Now, when you write a SAS program, you want to refer to a data set in the DEMO library. In this example, I am using the data set COFFEE, so you would reference it as: demo.coffee. Example as follows:

```
proc contents data=demo.coffee;
run;
```

When running that program, it will show the content of the data set coffee.

Another example for creating a library would be accessing tables stored in Oracle. The following is an example of how this can be accomplished. Oracle is just one example. The concept is the same for other databases as well.

Depending on the SAS/ACCESS products you have licensed, the syntax might look different.

As in the previous example, I must first create a library with a LIBNAME statement, here mydblib

```
LIBNAME mydblib oracle user=testuser password=testpass
path=schema_name;
```

When writing your program, you reference the library – mydblib – and the table in that library that you want to use. In this example, I would like to use a table called *Metadata*:

```
proc contents data=mydblib.metadata;
where dept="CSO";
run;
```

In summary, to access data or to make data available in SAS, you create libraries using the LIBNAME statement, pointing to a physical location. In the Appendix of this chapter, you will find link references.

Now let's turn to creating libraries in metadata.

Creating Libraries in SAS Metadata

In metadata, you, too, can create libraries that are referencing external data. You can do so by using the *Library Manager* in SAS Management Console or the *Library Manager* in SAS Environment Manager. The libraries that you create and the tables that you register are stored in your SAS Folders.

Creating libraries and registering data in metadata is recommended not only to make the data access for users from within clients easier and more monitorable; it is important when it comes to metadata security, logging, auditing etc.

Check out *Data by any other name*, which talks about data in Foundation and metadata, at: https://blogs.sas.com/content/sgf/2013/02/20/data-by-any-other-name/

One of the major benefits for creating libraries in metadata is the security aspect. You can tie down your environment in a way that is very easy to maintain. That is one of the reasons why we talked about users and groups in the previous chapter: you assign permissions to libraries via user groups. As you can see, we are building up to the chapter on metadata security.

Another great article about this topic is *Seeing SAS data through metadata*, https://blogs.sas.com/content/sgf/2013/03/06/seeing-sas-data-through-metadata/

SAS Folders and Libraries in SAS Metadata

The first step to creating libraries in metadata is to create a good folder structure that fits your users' needs and requirements.

Please see the Appendix for link references on SAS Folders

Quick recap: The folders are created under the *Folders* tab in SAS Management Console or in SAS Environment Manager. For now, until otherwise stated, I am using the Folders tab in SAS Management Console as shown in Figure 5.2. and I am creating my libraries using the *Library Manager* in SAS Management Console.

Figure 5.2: Folders in Library Manager

As mentioned prior, because libraries, tables and any other content you and your clients create are stored in these SAS folders, you want to make sure that you create a good folder structure. The libraries you create require for you to point to/to choose a SAS folder.

You will notice that I constantly repeat how important it is to implement a great folder structure.

I cannot stress that enough. Often, customers create folders that might not fit the company's needs or the users' needs, at all. Creating a SAS folder called *Dogs* for a library called *Cats*, for a group named *Hippo*, you must admit that this kinda defeats the purpose. Not only does it not make sense with respect to your groups, but it will also make your admin life a living hell. Imagine tons of folders and libraries and groups with names that make no sense whatsoever.

You might think "Does she think I am an idiot and don't know how to name a folder"? Au contraire! Trust me! But, I have seen problems and headaches due to weird names way too many times that I want to make sure you get the picture! It is so easy to be mired up in folders and more folders because there is no clear strategy in place to begin with. I have been there myself!

When we talked about groups in the prior chapter, I used an example that is based on the division I work in, *Customer Success*. Customer Success has a *director*, a team of *Systems Engineers*, *Customer Success Managers*, *Team Managers*, and *sub-teams*, which are based on *business units* each Customer Success Manager supports.

If we use this example, I would create a folder structure that fits this very department structure, as shown in Figure 5.3.

Figure 5.3: Customer Success Folder Structure

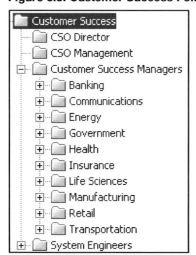

This folder structure is what I want to use for the libraries I am going to create. When we talk about metadata security later on, the SAS Folders are used to actually assign the permissions. Given that, you can see how important it is to have a good folder structure in place.

> **Note:** When I mention folders here, I always refer to SAS folders and never to file system folders.

Once you have created a good folder structure, you create your libraries.

Creating Libraries Continued

Let's continue with the Customer Success department example, simply to show you how the SAS folders, data registration, and libraries work in metadata. For this example, I am going to create a library that is called *CSO Management*. The data sets I want to register in that libraries are located on my local machine at:

```
C:\SAS\Data\Customer Success\CSO Management
```

If you are not already in SAS Management Console, log on as an administrator, then expand *Data Library Manager*. Right-click Libraries, *New*, as shown in Figure 5.4.

Figure 5.4: Creating a library in metadata

In the *New Library Wizard* window, choose a library template. Everything you see in the following figure (Figure 5.5), SAS can access. It shows only a snippet of the templates that you have available, there are many more. For our example, we will choose **SAS Base Library**.

Figure 5.5: New Library Wizard

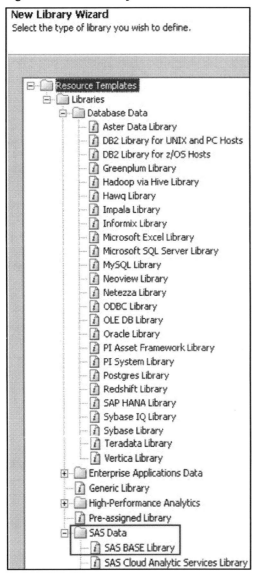

Next, you provide a name for the library, a description, a location – *location* is where the SAS Folders come into play. Here, the location is the metadata folder that you want to use to store the libraries and the tables in.

Figure 5.6: New library

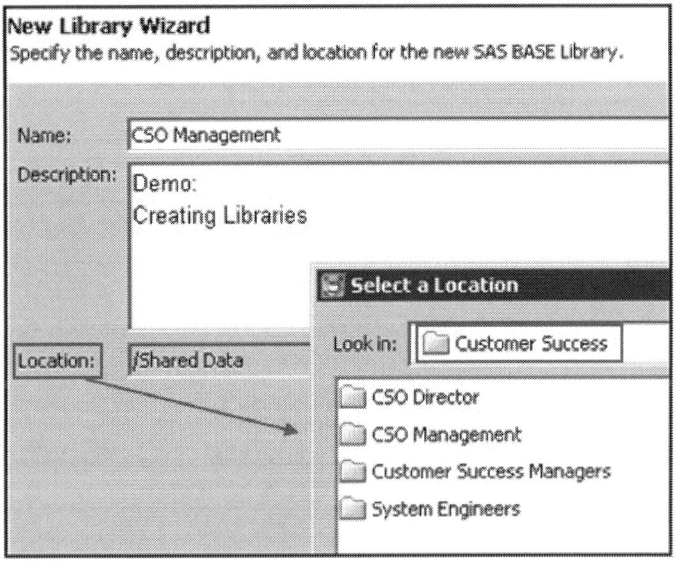

What I would like to highlight in Figure 5.6 is the location. It defaults to the SAS metadata folder *SharedData*. This is where you can now choose one of the folders that you created before. Going back to my example, my library in this example is called CSO Management, so, naturally, I am choosing the folder called CSO Management as my location.

> **Tip:** Please make sure you pay attention when adding the options in this window. It is so easy to quickly click through and to disregard the folder location.
>
> Having all your data end up in the Shared Data folder is of no avail. This is why it is a best practice to create a SAS folder structure before you start creating libraries in metadata.

The folder **Shared Data** is used to share content amongst users or groups. You can create sub folders to organize shared data more precisely. You do not have to use the Shared Data folder and can certainly create custom folders to be used for shared data.

> **Note:** The Share Data – or any other folders that are meant as shared location for that matter – should not be used as the general storage for all your libraries and tables, reports, projects etc.

Some customers prefer to create the SAS folders during the library creation, during the step when you choose a location, others prefer to put a folder structure in place before actually creating any libraries. I believe the latter is the better approach. It is easy to lose sight of what has to be created and what has already been created. It's certainly up to you which strategy you choose. Your goal should always be to create a structure that makes sense for you, your users. Not only does it simply make sense, but it also makes your admin life easier. And, another thought: If you leave the company, or, you inherit an environment someone else has created, it is so much easier when you have the benefit of a well set up environment.

Let's get back to creating the library. After choosing a name and the folder location, hit *Next*. Now you must choose a SAS Application Server for the library to be affiliated with. (Chapter 2, SAS Architecture, covers the SAS workspace server, in case you need a refresher.)

A SAS Workspace Server fulfills client requests for SAS sessions. When a user logs on to, let's say, SAS Enterprise Guide, and accesses a data set within a SAS library, the user does that "on" a Workspace Server. The workspace server is a single-user server process. The user uses the server, and then disconnects. The default application server is **SASApp** (as shown in figure 5.7), which refers to the default SAS Workspace Server that is automatically created during the SAS installation. Choosing SASApp means that your users' jobs are executed on the default SAS workspace server.

Figure 5.7: Choosing an application server

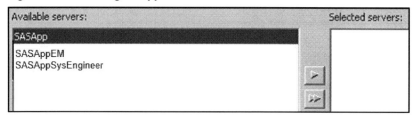

As you can see in Figure 5.7, in addition to *SASApp* server, there is a *SASAppEM* and a *SASAppSysEngineer*. For the purpose of this example, I want certain user groups to run their jobs on their respective workspace servers. All jobs System Engineers submit are running on the dedicated application server called *SASAppSysEngineers*. With that dedicated server, and the appropriate permissions, no one will be able to access libraries for the Systems Engineers other than the System Engineers themselves (and the SAS admin of course)

If you look at the left top corner of Figure 5.8, below, you see *Libref*. The *Libref* is the name for the library in metadata. When you start creating a library, you enter a name for the library. A libref is a nickname for the library.

The name has to be one-to eight characters long, and the first character must be a letter or an underscore ( ). All other characters can be either letters or numbers. The libref name cannot contain spaces. For this library, I chose *CSOMg* as libref.

In the next step of our example, we will select the default application server *SASApp* by moving it to the right (SASApp instead of the *SASAppSysEngineer* App Server*)*. Hit *Next*. Now you are choosing a *Libref* and the path to your physical location where the data resides. The physical location is your file system, as shown in Figure 5.8.

Figure 5.8: Choosing data location

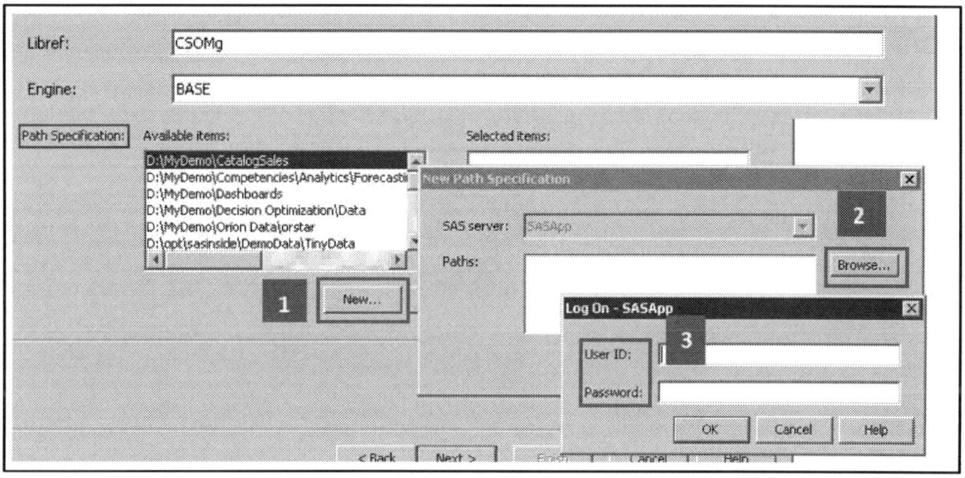

Because the location (here, the location refers to the file system where your data is actually located) does not yet appear in the *Available Items*, I click *New*, then *Browse*. That opens a login window where you are asked to enter a physical user ID, meaning, you cannot use an internal account. An internal account is only known to SAS. When we use the application server, we refer to a workspace server. Spawning a workspace server requires a user ID that is an external account. In this case, I am using my user ID, Anja, which is a physical account.

Once you chose the file system path where your data resides, click *Next*, examine it to see whether it looks good and *Finish*.

If you now look under *Library Manager*, you will find the library *CSO Management*. Right now, the metadata library is empty, because the physical file system tables have not yet been registered in metadata. So, as a next step, you must register tables. Registering tables simply means that you bring the tables that you want into metadata. Right-click CSO *Management* library, *Register Tables*. The following window appears, as shown in Figure 5.9.

Figure 5.9: SAS library

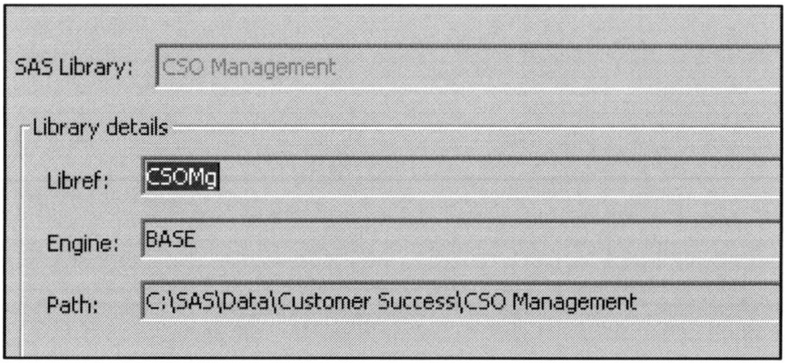

You can see CSO Management is the SAS Library, and CSOMg is the libref. Engine shows BASE because that is what we chose when we created the library. The path points to the file system location that we specified when we created the library.

In the next window, you will now see all the data sets that are stored in
`C:\SAS\Data\Customer Success\CSO Management`

Figure 5.10: SAS Data Sets

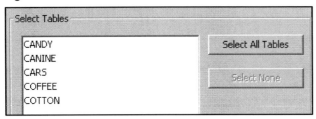

You can either select all tables, or, you can just choose one or two. Recall when we talked about SAS LIBNAME statements at the beginning of this chapter, and how you create libraries. When you use those LIBNAME statements, you can only see all of the data in the specified location. In metadata, even though you, too, see all the tables in this file location, you can choose explicitly which tables to register. This is a great option, especially for environments without a clear system folder structure. It's a great option to choose tables for certain purposes only.

Select the tables that you want and click *Finish*. Now your metadata library shows metadata tables. Switching to the Folders tab, you will see that the library and the tables appear in the folder that we created before, as shown in Figure 5.11.

Figure 5.11: CSO Management folder's content

Let's go back to the Plug-ins tab in SAS Management Console, Library Manager. If you right-click on the CSO Management library, then do a Display LIBNAME Statement, you'll see the following - shown in Figure 5.12.

Figure 5.12. Generated LIBNAME statement in metadata

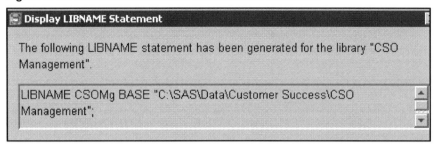

Looks familiar? You could copy this LIBNAME statement and run it in SAS Enterprise Guide. You would assign a library called CSOMg (our libref) and you would see all the tables you see in SAS Management Console, Library Manager for that library.

Note: this is not available for pre-assigned libraries.

Aside from the registering tables difference, another difference between libname statements submitted in a display manager vs creating libraries in metadata is that the libraries that you create via LIBNAME statement in a SAS client are temporary, that means, when you close the session and start a new one, you have to assign the LIBNAME statement again. Users have the option though to set the library properties to permanent, which would make the library available whenever you start a SAS client. However, you still have each table in the library available.

From a security perspective, you must put permissions in place on the operating system to make sure your users can only get to the tables that they ought to see when submitting the LIBNAME statement. In metadata, you can set the security with grants or denies on the folder level, library level, table level, and with that, apply an additional security layer.

The administration of data, access, permissions, is much easier in metadata than on the OS only. To make sure we can use the full benefit of creating libraries in metadata, we should create users and groups in metadata. Do you see how it all starts to come together?

Metadata Library Troubleshooting

If you receive an error while creating the library or when registering tables, one of the first things to check is

1. Whether you are logged on as admin user.
2. If the user ID that you are using when prompted during the creation and registration process is a physical account and not an internal SAS account.
3. That you have Read and Write permissions, so you can access the physical tables.

For pre-assigned libraries, if you run into a situation where you know for a fact that pre-assigned libraries have been set up, yet they are not used, make sure the OBJECTSERVERPARMS system option is not set to NOPREASSIGNMENT. The NOPREASSIGNMENT applies to all SAS servers that are started by the object spawner. The

OBJECTSERVERPARMS system option can be used in a configuration file that is used to start the metadata server.

Also, in case of any problems during library creation or registering tables, check the log files to see whether there is any indication why a problem occurred:

Metadata Server log:

Windows: `Lev1\SASMeta\MetadataServer\Logs`

UNIX: `Lev1/SASMeta/MetadataServer/Logs`

Object Spawner log:

Windows: `Lev1\ObjectSpawner\Logs`

UNIX: `Lev1/ObjectSpawner/Logs`

Pre-Assigned Libraries

We talked about creating libraries via LIBNAME statements and in metadata using the Library Manager. You can also pre-assign libraries and make them available for users as soon as they start to use the associated SAS server.

As we learned in the architecture chapter, application servers (such as a workspace server) are used when for example, a user in SAS Enterprise Guide makes a request to run a job that uses metadata etc. If the application server that is being used has a pre-assigned library assigned to it, then that library will automatically get pre-assigned.

When you pre-assign libraries in metadata, you have to choose an option, a type, in which they are pre-assigned. The options are:

- Using the native engine, which is Base SAS.
- Metadata LIBNAME engine.
- By external configuration.

The differences between the pre-assignment types are the way security is handled and whether configuration files must be created or modified.

Amongst other differences, the most profound difference between the native engine and metadata library engine is the way the permissions are checked. The native engine still contacts the metadata server. However, it disregards the data level authorization permissions read, write, delete, and create.

Before creating pre-assigned libraries, consider the following: too many pre-assigned libraries might slow down the process in which the data will be available to your users, because there might be an initialization delay for the workspace server.

The paper, *Tracking Down the Culprit of a SAS Workspace Server Initialization Delay*, provides some great input on pre-assigned libraries and how they can slow down the workspace server initialization and other delays. Check out pages 3 to 9, available at: https://www.sas.com/content/dam/SAS/support/en/sas-global-forum-proceedings/2018/2003-2018.pdf

Pre-Assignment or No-Pre-Assignment?

Have I mentioned that there are always exceptions to a rule? If your users – for example – need to run hand written code in SAS Enterprise Guide, pre-assigned libraries might make sense because in this scenario, a library assignment would not work as on-demand. This could cause calls where users complain that they cannot get to their data, or, you would have to teach your users how to assign libraries. This is one reason why you might want to pre-assign more libraries.

As with everything, please consider carefully and make sure you have a proper planning. Remember: You can have too much of a good thing.

Metadata-Bound Libraries

In addition to libraries that you create in metadata, I would like to add another library creation option into the mix: the metadata-bound libraries.

A metadata-bound library is a physical library that is tied to a metadata library. When you create metadata-bound libraries, a new metadata object is created, which then binds the physical library to that object. It's a nice way to close loopholes. Put another way: think of a metadata-bound library as a key. A metadata-bound library locks up the physical tables with a key that is stored in metadata. With that, if someone wants to use the data, they must go to the metadata server to get the key.

You might be wondering why we need metadata-bound libraries since our metadata libraries are associated with physical data anyhow. Let's take a step back and look at the LIBNAME scenarios that we discussed so far. You can code a LIBNAME statement to assign a library that points to all the tables in that physical location, or, preferably, create a library in metadata.

Consider the following situation: A user creates a project in SAS Enterprise Guide, using tables that you registered in a metadata library. You know that metadata permissions to your metadata libraries and metadata tables are assigned via SAS metadata folders, and therefore, should apply to this user. You want your user to have access to specific tables only. Well, the user accesses ALL the data in the library, even though you explicitly denied access to certain tables. This is puzzling, isn't it? Here is what happened: Even though you created the library in metadata, the user assigned a LIBNAME statement in SAS Enterprise Guide by running, for example: **LIBNAME CSOMg "c:\sas\data\CSO\Management**. If a user knows where data is located, metadata can be bypassed. If no filesystem permissions are assigned, the user has free access to all data. And this is where metadata-bound libraries come into play.

Since pictures often say more than words, take a look at Figure 5.13 to see a visual depiction of the scenario just described.

Figure 5.13: Access to Traditional versus Metadata-Bound Tables

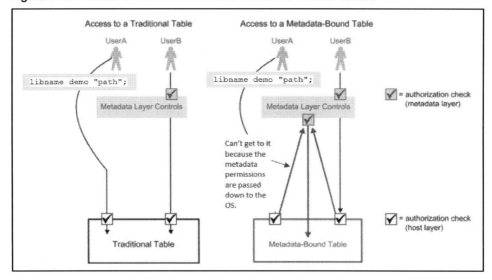

In Figure 5.13, UserA accesses the data directly (via LIBNAME statement) and UserB requests data through a SAS client that uses metadata libraries. With a metadata-bound library, user A – or generally all users for that matter - cannot bypass metadata permissions. So, if the user tries to access the physical data directly (after successfully passing through the host layer controls) they are redirected to the metadata server where the metadata layer controls are also enforced.

To learn about metadata-bound libraries, how they are used and how they are created, check out:

Closing the "LIBNAME loophole" with metadata-bound libraries, at:
https://blogs.sas.com/content/sasdummy/2013/12/24/metadata-bound-libraries/

This blog is written in an earlier SAS release but applies to SAS 9.4 as well.

You can find additional resources in the Appendix.

Summary

Creating libraries in metadata and registering physical data in libraries can make your admin life easier. Consider your environment, your users' needs, the data that you want to make available to your users, before implementing libraries. Think about if pre-assigned libraries might make sense in your environment. Consider metadata-bound libraries to tie up the environment. There is a lot of information available to read and to study. This chapter will help you lay down a foundation.

Chapter 6: SAS 9.4 Metadata Security

Introduction

The trouble with security is that you can never tell if it's good until it's too late. Think about the following scenario: imagine that you have the option to protect your cell phone data by using a PIN or a finger print – depending on the models you have (new versus old), a retina scan, or nothing at all. You have contacts stored, WhatsApps and texts, emails, saved credit cards (heaven forbid) and so on.

If you don't use any of the authorization mechanisms, let's just hope you will never lose your cell phone. If you use a PIN, the authorization strength pretty much depends on the numbers and letters you choose for your password. Famous example: password 1234567.and the like. With this, your password would be easy to crack. If your password looks like 17353820168302, (just an example) the password strength is much higher.

With a finger print authentication, you clearly have a much stronger authorization mechanism than with numbers. Eye recognition: As long as no one steals your eyeballs, retina scans would be a great and tied security feature to protect your contacts, texts, saved credit card information, pictures, and everything else stored on your phone. Considering all this, let's turn our attention to security in SAS. It's the same concept, same principles!

Your contacts, emails, texts, and pictures etc. are like your SAS metadata assets (data, libraries, reports, users etc.). You can choose to not secure your environment at all, you can implement authorization mechanisms that are a bit stronger (the numbers to unlock your cell), or, you can lock down and protect your assets with your life – so to speak. For SAS, this means you implement a concept in which granting and denying requests are carefully considered, always making sure your

SAS 9.4 security covers the following:

- Authentication
- Authorization
- Encryption

That is a lot of ground to cover. Our main focus in this chapter is authorization in SAS.

Authentication is of course important too. Internal authentication mechanisms unify the SAS realm and provide a degree of independence from your general computing environment. The internal mechanisms are SAS internal authentication and SAS token authentication. External authentication mechanisms integrate SAS into your computing environment. External mechanisms include direct LDAP authentication, host authentication (credential-based), Integrated Windows authentication, and web authentication.

Credential management provides single sign-on through reuse of cached credentials or retrieval of stored passwords. Pluggable authentication modules (PAM) extend UNIX host authentication and trust relationships facilitate communication to the metadata server by permitting one privileged account to connect on behalf of other users (trusted user) or by accepting requests that use a proprietary protocol (trusted peer).

For more information about SAS authentication, see the Appendix for this chapter.

As for encryption, in SAS there are two classes of encryption strength available:

For compatibility with legacy systems, SASProprietary encoding is supported. This method is available in all deployments and is appropriate for preventing accidental exposure of information.

For a higher level of security, it is recommended to use industry-standard encryption and hashing algorithms. These methods provide stronger protection and are available in all deployments, except where prohibited by import restrictions.

SAS recommends that you use the strongest security standards available for your environment.

Now let's turn our attention to authorization.

Authorization

Chapter 4 in this book covered users and groups, and talked about the goal of creating those, and the idea of why groups might be better than administering and managing each individual user.

In this chapter, we will take it further and talk about permissions for the users and groups that you created.

The Appendix of this chapter provides you with a link to documentation for User and Group Management in case you'd need to look into it further.

What Does *Authorization* Mean?

Let's start out by defining what authorization actually is.

Authorization is a security mechanism which is used to determine users' or groups' permissions on objects: file system, data, documents, projects, and so on. The authorization process comes after the authentication process, meaning, after the system verifies that you are who you say you are, it checks whether permissions are assigned for you and either grants or denies access to the resources that you are trying to access. You can use role-based permissions for users and groups. Authorization could also be based on authentication mechanisms such as Active Directory or LDAP.

For SAS, this means protecting your metadata assets: SAS folders, metadata libraries and metadata tables, etc.

You have different persona groups in your company: some must work with sensitive data, some do the scheduling, users write programs, admins who administer the SAS environment, some users might work with Oracle data while other use Hadoop. Because you have different personas with different needs, your goal should be to protect your environment appropriately, to grant or deny appropriately.

Interface to Apply Permissions

The access to an object for a user or a group is assigned in the authorization properties of the metadata object. An example: In SAS Management Console, Folders tab, right-click on a folder, *Properties*, *Authorization* tab, as shown in Figure 6.1.

Figure 6.1: SAS Management Console Folder Properties

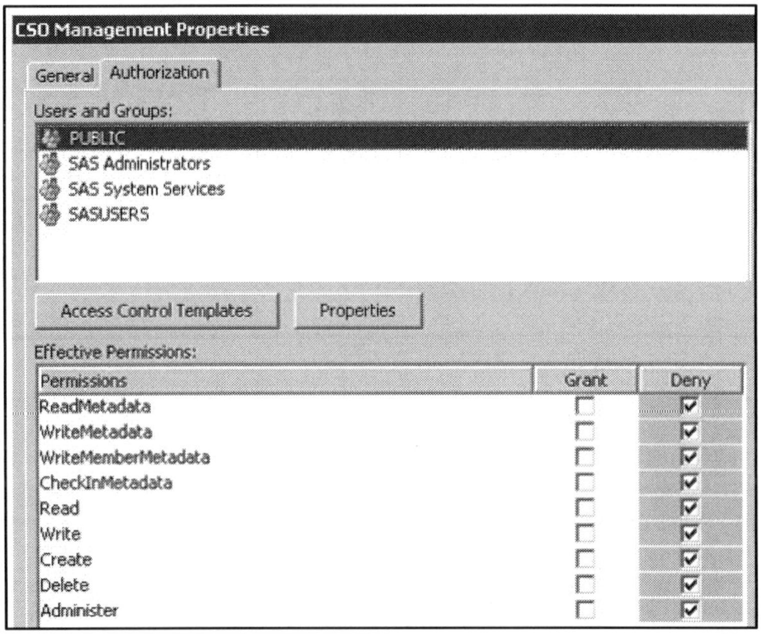

The default identities and groups you typically see in an initial install are:

- PUBLIC and SASUSERS (implicit SAS groups)
- SAS Systems Services
- SAS Administrators
- SAS Administrator

As a refresher: PUBLIC includes every OS/LDAP/AD authenticated user with our without a metadata identity. SASUSERS includes every OS/LDAP/AD authenticated user with metadata identity. All members of the SASUSERS group are also members of the PUBLIC group. The closest (and only) listed group for an unregistered user is PUBLIC. The closest listed group for a registered user is often SASUSERS.

SAS Administrators is a group with the unrestricted user sasadm@saspw as initial and only member in this group. You can use this group to add yourself and other SAS admins. SAS Administrator is the unrestricted users with the login ID sasadm@saspw). The closest listed group for an administrator is usually SAS Administrators.SAS Systems Services group's member is the SAS Trusted Users (display name). It is an internal account user-ID called sastrust@saspw. A user ID used for trusted connections.

Authorization and PUBLIC and SASUSERS

Let's take a look at the implicit groups PUBLIC and SASUSERS from an authorization perspective.

Public

The general rule is that you should deny Public permissions to your metadata. The reason for this general rule is that you do not want users without a metadata identity to access your metadata objects, such as tables, libraries and more. An analogy could be that you do not want to have strangers in your house.

There are always exceptions to a rule. If, and only if, you want to set up your environment with public access, and if, and only if, it makes sense for your environment, public access might be considered. Just opening up your environment by granting all users access to avoid having to set up permissions, is not a good practice – at all. Please be considered and think about the consequences a wide open environment could have.

Later in this chapter, we will go into more details, describing different options to implement permissions, using Public. For this introduction, let's keep it simple.

SASUSERS

Initially, when SAS is deployed, SASUSERS is typically assigned the baseline permissions ReadMetadata and WriteMetadata automatically.

You might think: Why do I want to have a WriteMetadata for SASUSERS? Doesn't that mean that everyone in metadata can create objects? Hypothetically, you are right, but you usually wouldn't necessarily change it immediately.

The general rule – or, better put – the way many customers use the permissions in SAS is that they leave the grant for ReadMetadata as is for SASUSERS, for exactly that reason: users have to see the metadata in order to touch them. It can be one way to knock out the individual ReadMetadata by simply using the ReadMetadata for all objects in the Foundation repository. This is considered broad access.

Of course, there are always exceptions to the rule, and there might be situations where denying ReadMetadata might make sense.

We will address the SASUSERS group and best practices later in this chapter, and you will learn about different scenarios for using SASUSERS.

For the purpose of this introduction, remember the general rule: we want to close the door to any type of metadata objects for PUBLIC, and can use – if applicable – the ReadMetadata permissions broadly for all objects. This is the ground rule.

Because SAS is a powerful software with lots of features, there is much more to the ground rule and many more options and features are available to you to implement permission patterns.

An analogy here could be: you have the latest and greatest cell phone . You can either just turn it on and use it as is, without even locking it with at least a simple password, or, you protect your cell phone and educate yourself about the different options that you have available to actually protect it in the best way possible. We will address all this later on in this chapter. Don't get tired of my "we will discuss it later in this chapter". You will see how it will all nicely tie into each other and how it makes all sense.

Permissions in SAS

To perform any task such as reading a table, updating or deleting objects in metadata, your users must have appropriate access. At the same time, you might want to protect certain metadata objects, making sure that your users have only access to metadata objects that they are supposed to access and have available. Here are the permissions that you have available and that are used in SAS:

- **ReadMetadata** allows your users to see an object. If users do not have the ReadMetadata permissions and the effective grant for ReadMetadata, the objects are simply not visible.

- **WriteMetadata** enables users to update or delete an object, such as a table or library.

- **WriteMemberMetadata** allows users to add or delete objects within a folder. They cannot touch (delete, rename etc.) the folder itself, unless they have an effective grant for WriteMetadata.

- **CheckInMetadata** is used to indirectly modify objects in the Foundation repository, by checking the object out into a project repository. That way, metadata can be conveniently modified and checked back into the Foundation repository afterward. This is a great option to avoid interference when working with metadata objects. The CheckInMetadata permission is solely used for SAS Data Integration Studio.

Aside from the general permissions, SAS also has specialized permissions, for example, Read, Write, Create, and so on. For the purpose of the book, we won't cover the specialized permissions. They are described in the SAS Security Guide: Specialized Permissions in SAS. The link to the documentation is available in the Appendix of this chapter.

Access Controls in SAS

Still with me?

There are two direct controls of permissions in SAS:

Direct Control Explicit (aka ACE) and Direct Control via *Access Control Template* (ACTs).

Access Control Entries (ACEs)**: direct permissions.**

One way to assign permissions in metadata is to simply add a group or a user to a metadata object (such as a folder) and assign permission to that group or user.

Access Control Templates (ACTs)**: patterned access**.

With an ACT you apply permission patterns with grants or denies.

So, rather than individually checking grants or denies for x amount of groups, you put the permissions required together and create a pattern, which you then apply to the metadata object, such as a folder.

An analogy here could be: I want to treat a GROUP of friends for a dinner in a nice restaurant. I can either take every friend (user) individually on different days, letting them eat and drink whatever they want (permissions – individual), or, I simply take them all (group), and we all go at the same time and eat and drink from the menu together – as a group (control pattern). An Access Control Entry (ACE) is used to apply grant or deny for specific resources directly. That means, the grant or deny is unique to that metadata object, such a library or a folder. You can apply ACEs for individual users and groups (direct permissions).

Let's take a look at the default Access Control Templates SAS provides, and look at why this is easier to maintain. To view ACTs in SAS, go to SAS Management Console, Authorization Manager and expand Access Control Templates. as shown in Figure 6.2.

Figure 6.2: Authorization Manager

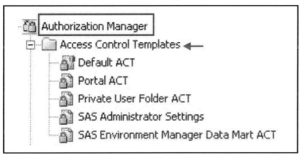

The *Default ACT*, aka repository ACT, is the metadata server's initial permission template, that includes SASUSERS and PUBLIC, System Services, SAS Administrators.

When you start SAS Management Console and log on with a user ID, this is the initial permission setting the metadata server is going by, as shown in Figure 6.3.

Figure 6.3: Access Control Template Properties.

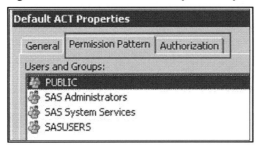

If you look at the properties of an Access Control Template, you will notice a *Permission Pattern* Tab and an *Authorization* tab. If you look at the properties of, let's say, a folder, you only have an Authorization tab: The *Authorization* tab in an Access Control Template defines who can change, modify or delete that specific Access Control Template; In the *Permission Pattern* tab, you add the users or groups that you want to grant or deny permissions to metadata objects when that ACT is applied, such as a metadata folder, a library, an Enterprise Guide project, and so forth. The permissions on individual objects do not need this, and therefore, you only have *Authorization*.

Going back to why it is easier to maintain an Access Control Template than individual permissions for groups or users on an actual metadata object: if permission change would be necessary, or, users or groups must be added or removed, you simply must go to the Authorization Manager and make the change in that respective Access Control Template. With individual permission in objects itself you will have to go to that specific object and change it there. Because of this, SAS tends to recommend using Access Control Templates. But – wait for it – there are always exceptions.to the rule. Individual permissions on objects for personas might be an option for your particular environment.

In the best practice section later in this book, we will talk about ACTs and ACEs. The goal is to provide you with as many ideas and rules and recommendations as possible, to enable you to choose what is best for you.

When implementing permissions, it is always important to keep in mind that there is a *permission inheritance*. All metadata objects inherit and pass on permissions to objects in one way or the other, for example:

Figure 6.4: Inheritance Paths

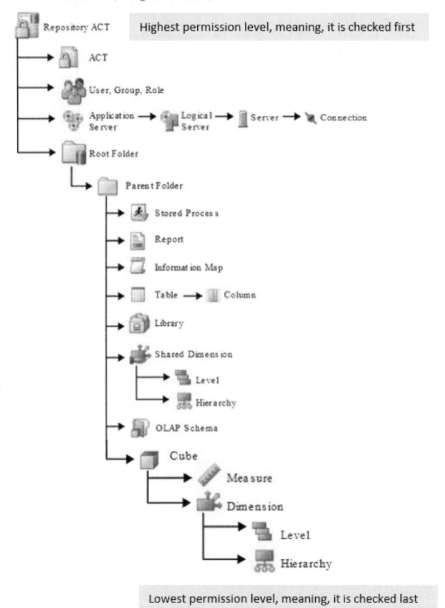

Source: SAS Security Administration Guide at
https://go.documentation.sas.com/?docsetId=bisecag&docsetTarget=p0eqebtrv1qhzhn1qje3k
ytr5kcr.htm&docsetVersion=9.4&locale=en

You will notice the shaded boxes, referring to "Highest to Lowest,". This simply means: the parent object that passes down permissions to every object in the Foundation repository, is an Access Control Template. Per default, it is the DefaultACT, and so forth.

The following graph shows how object inheritance works:

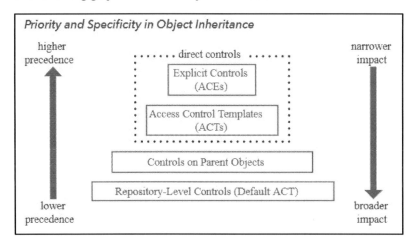

When we talk about inheritance, object inheritance, we need to address *identity hierarchy* as well as one doesn't go without the other. Identity follows a certain ranking and its hierarchy affects authorization decisions as seen below. (Resource: https://go.documentation.sas.com/?docsetId=bisecag&docsetTarget=n00yrb8qwmxdm2n1axb oebwf72u3.htm&docsetVersion=9.4&locale=en)

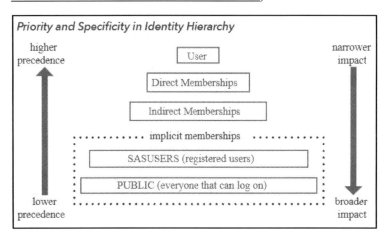

Identity follows a certain ranking and its hierarchy affects authorization decisions. Here is how the precedence works:

1. Users' individual and successfully authenticated identity is checked.
2. A group that has the user as a direct member. This is a first-level group membership for the user.

3. A group that has another user group as a direct member. For example, assume that the user belongs to a group named ETL_Advanced, and that group is a member of another group called ETL_Basic. In that case, the ETL_Basic group is a second-level group (indirect membership) for that user. If you have additional levels of nesting, each successive level has less precedence.

4. The SASUSERS implicit group, which includes everyone who has an individual identity.

5. The PUBLIC implicit group, which includes everyone who can access the metadata server (regardless of whether they have an individual identity or not).

Table 6.1: Example of Identity Hierarchies

Scenario	User's Identity Hierarchy
User has no individual identity	Primary identity: PUBLIC
User has an identity and no explicit group memberships	Primary Identity: self First-level membership: SASUSERS Second-level membership: PUBLIC
User is a direct member of GroupA and GroupB GroupA is a member of the Report Users group	Primary identity: self First-level memberships: GroupA, GroupB Second-level membership: Report Users Third-level membership: SASUSERS Fourth-level membership: PUBLIC

Understanding inheritance is important for troubleshooting. Whenever you run into a problem such as, you know you assigned a ReadMetadata on an object, but the user cannot see it, it is helpful and makes things easier when you understand how objects inherit and how identities fall into the mix.

There is one rule that does not allow for any exceptions:

Do not make PUBLIC or SASUSERS a member of another group.

PUBIC and SASUSERS can be members of roles and can be used for creating Access Control Templates.

Explanation:

If you make PUBLIC a member of Group A, then a user who is an indirect member of Group A has Group A as his lowest precedence membership. All users are automatically members of PUBLIC. So, with the scenario we just described, we contradict the rule that every users' lowest membership is in fact PUBLIC. Of course, hypothetically it could be done. Let's just say: the recommendation is not to do it.

You still with me? I am hammering you with lots of information right now, stay with me here.

If you don't follow best practices, then this can be a key source of hard to understand permission conflicts. More resources can be found in the Appendix, including an article written by Paul Homes, which is a great example of how permission settings could go wrong, and how to fix it. Of special interest are slides 15 and 16, where he talks about wide denials and narrow grants.

Now we have checked off the ACEs and ACTs and inheritance, let's move on to the next important topic in the metadata permission world: the colour coding.

Color Coding

It is a bit like with traffic lights: Green, we can go, yellow we better hurry (proceed with caution), red, we stop. In SAS, too, we use colors – not red or yellow, but we do use white, gray and green. It is to help you recognize which type of permissions you have assigned to your metadata objects, and where it inherits its permissions from.

In SAS, the colors have the following meaning:

- White background: A permission has been explicitly assigned for a user or a group on a specific metadata object, such as a metadata SAS folder.

- Green background: An Access Control Template has been directly assigned to a metadata object, again, such as a metadata folder.

- Gray background: Permission is inherited from a parent object or a parent identity. For example: a white check box for PUBLIC for a denial for ReadMetadata on the object (such as a folder) will show as a gray check box for ReadMetadata denial for SASUSERS on the same object (unless it is overridden with an ACT or ACE). Remember the identity and object inheritance graph earlier?

Shown in Figure 6.5, you can see how the color coding looks like:

Figure 6.5: Color Coding Example

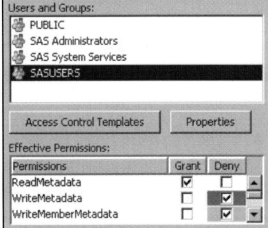

Example

In Chapter 4 – Data and Library Administration – we created libraries, SAS folders and registered tables in metadata, using the Customer Success Organization, CSO for short.

First, let's look at the SAS folders in metadata, expand Customer Success, and highlight CSO Management. This is the folder for storing metadata content for all our managers, shown in Figure 6.6.

Figure 6.6: CSO Management Folder Structure

If we look at this folder and its contents from an inheritance perspective, the library CSO Management and the tables Candy, Canine, Cars, Coffee and Cotton, inherit the permissions from the folder CSO Management.

From a permission perspective (in its simplest form): if a user tries to access a table in this folder, suppose the table Coffee, the metadata server checks for these things:

Are there any ACEs applied for users or groups, are there any ACT templates applied, are permissions inherited? Again, in its simplest form, we can say that an ACE takes precedence over an Access Control Template. Later, when we look at some of the examples and best practice, you will find that it is pretty much all black and white.

You will find that there is always a definitive predictable effective permission result. Make sure you really understand the effective permission decision. With that, you will be able to apply the permissions in a way that fits your SAS environment. Understanding permission decisions is very helpful when it comes to troubleshooting as you can easier follow the paths of where the problem might lay.

In the following section, I would like to provide you with some best practices and rules for metadata security model design. The models discussed here have been implemented successfully at many sites. But – wait for it – there are always exceptions to the rules!

Even though the model below has been successfully implemented at many sites, it does not necessarily mean that it is a good fit for you. Please do not just take it and simply apply it to your environment. Implementing security requires careful and thoughtful planning, a lot of consideration. If you have a complex environment, sit down with a pen and paper and draw out your environment.

First and foremost, make sure you are well educated and informed about the subject. Ensure you know the concepts well and have a clear idea of what work you will have to do: how many metadata server environments do you have to consider, what personas do you have, what data has to be available for your users, what type of work do they do, what kind of SAS metadata folder structure would make sense for your SAS environment, etc.

As an added bonus, planning provides a great opportunity to do some spring cleaning: do you have users that are not with the company anymore and whose user IDs are just "hanging around". Do you have any redundancy when it comes to data. How about your file system folder structure, etc.

Do not try to design or implement a security model until you know what goals it must achieve. This is the most important thing. Sometimes there are situations where a security concept has been implemented that does not make sense because it does not fit the requirements and needs.

We have now covered the basic fundamentals. Time to take you through some best practice and examples!

Best Practice: The Golden Rules for Metadata Security Model Design

The best practice and tips that we will discuss here are based on many contributors' work and experiences worldwide, including Cecily Hoffritz, Johannes Jørgensen and David Stern. Cecily is a Principal Business Solutions Manager and Johannes is a Senior Principal Consultant, both from the SAS Denmark office and specialize in metadata security. David Stern, who is a Principal Technical Architect in the SAS Global Enablement and Learning (GEL) team, specializes in SAS administration, authorization and migration. The following section will provide you with some great guidance that will help you with metadata security implementation considerations. In the following best practice and rules, the main focus will be on Access Control Templates.

To make sure you can implement the rules suggested, let's first review how to create ACTs.

Creating Custom Access Control Templates

In the SAS Management Console, logon as the unrestricted admin user sasadm@saspw, or use an admin ID that has the capabilities and permissions to create metadata and work with security objects.

1. In SAS Management Console, expand the *Authorization Manager* plug-in.
2. Right click on Access Control Template, New.

The rule for custom ACTs is generally that it includes PUBLIC and SASUSERS, both denied everything, also including SAS System Services and the SAS Administrator group.

> **Note:** You do not have to create an ACT for SAS Administrators. SAS provides that per default. SAS Administrators can have all permissions granted, SAS System Services get a ReadMetadata.

Now create our first ACT and call it ***Public and SASUSERS Denied***.

Add the following members to this ACT:

SASUSERS and PUBLIC

SAS Administrators

SAS System Services

Assign permissions as followed:

SASUSERS and PUBLIC: **deny** ReadMetadata and **deny** WriteMetadata (**deny** everything)!

SAS Administrators: **grant** for everything

SAS System Services: **grant** for ReadMetadata

> **IMPORTANT:** When you create an ACT that includes a deny for PUBLIC and SASUSERS, you must also add the SAS Administrators group and SAS System Services to this custom ACT. This is extremely important! Please always keep in mind:
>
> PUBLIC includes all authenticated users without a metadata identity.
>
> SASUSERS includes all authenticated users with a metadata identity. Every user in metadata is member of PUBLIC and SASUSERS.
>
> Every user in metadata is member of PUBLIC and SASUSERS until explicitly added to a custom ACT that grants certain permissions.
>
> In an ACT that has a deny for PUBLIC and SASUSERS, you lock out EVERY user, including the SAS administrators. It is for that reason that you ALWAYS must add the SAS Administrators to every ACT that you create. The unrestricted user sasadm@saspw is an exception. This user will not be locked out because it is unrestricted.

We will use the *PUBLIC SASUSERS Denied* ACT later.

Rule 1: If Applicable, Use Access Control Templates (ACT) and Avoid Using Access Control Entries (ACE) Whenever Possible

This is always an interesting discussion amongst us SAS metadata security nerds. Many insist that ACTs must be used at all time and that ACEs must not be used ever. I would not put it that strictly, because – wait for it – there are always exceptions to the rule. It's a bit like telling you to never to eat canned food (choosing that example cause my pantry is full of ravioli cans), but, one day, you simply do not have anything else to eat, so, here you go. Canned food doesn't look that bad after all. You get the idea.

Why are ACTs recommended? If you only apply ACTs and no ACEs, your job as an administrator will be much easier because you can maintain all security changes centrally in the *Authorization Manager* plug-in of SAS Management Console. Remember, the goal should always be to make it as easy as possible for you and to find the best way to maintain your SAS users easily.

The security design behind row level security on information maps and cubes forces you to apply ACEs. There are no other exceptions where applying ACEs would be necessary.

Some exceptions to the rule apply, such as when SAS is deployed, some ACEs are already applied to certain objects by the SAS deployment wizard. Also, the security design behind row level security on information maps and cubes forces you to apply ACEs. Do not change these. There are no other exceptions where applying ACEs would be necessary.

Rule 2: Only Add Groups to Access Control Templates (ACTs)

As a best practice, add only groups to each ACT and include the group name in the ACT name.

Going back to the example that I used throughout: an ACT for the Customer Success organization could have an ACT called CSO Managers, another ACT could be named CSO System Engineers and so forth.

You can go further such as providing the type of access as part of the name.

Explanation: It is much less effort to maintain your security model for groups rather than for individual users. If you only use groups in your ACTs, you can grant users the permissions that they need by placing them in the appropriate groups. You can change a user's permissions by changing the groups that they belong to, far more easily than by removing that user from several ACTs (or worse, removing their ACEs, if you can even find them!) and then adding that user to new ACTs.

Important for LDAP Synchronized Groups:

Take adequate precautions when you work with LDAP synchronized groups. If you automatically synchronize groups into metadata from LDAP, using something like the bulk-load macros, do not add such groups to an ACT, except if you are 100% certain that these groups won't be deleted. Please take adequate precaution!

If groups in LDAP are deleted, yet they are still active groups in SAS, being assigned to an ACT, when the synchronization is running, your groups in metadata will be deleted. So, what is deleted in LDAP and then synchronized with SAS, will be deleted in SAS metadata as well. This is very important to understand. I would like to highlight an article from David Stern on the SAS Administration and Deployment Community : https://communities.sas.com/t5/SAS-Communities-Library/Shadow-Groups-for-LDAP-Synchronisation/ta-p/373540, including the comment at the end from Paul Homes.

Rule 3: ACTs Only Grant Access to Explicit Groups, Never Deny

This rule is the most important rule of all! If you follow rule 1 and rule 2 and you only use ACTs as recommended, you must not deny any permissions to any group - – except PUBLIC or SASUSERS.

Explanation: Following this rule guarantees that your security model cannot suffer from permission conflicts. Avoiding permission conflicts is extremely important if you want to keep your sanity. A permission conflict occurs when conflicting settings (at least one grant and at least one deny), for a permission such as read metadata, directly apply to the same metadata object for where a user is a direct member of both groups. It's a bit like a kid asking each parent if it is ok to eat an entire bucket of candy on Halloween. The dad grants permission, but the mom is saying no, listing all the bad things that could happen to the stomach. There you have it: conflicting permissions.

Using our CSO Management folder example again: If user Benji is a direct member of the CSO Management group with an ACT that grants access to the CSO Management folder, yet there is another ACT, called Systems Engineers with the same permissions to the Systems Engineers group, and Benji happens to be a direct member of the Systems Engineer group, he won't be able to access the folder, because the permission is conflicting. A user that has a direct grant and a direct deny on the same object, such as a folder, would be denied access. In that instance, a deny always takes precedence over a grant.

This is the general rule. It's a different story when we bring in users who are in a group that is a member of another group – so in that case, we have direct versus indirect membership and the permissions concept would work differently.

For the example with the CSO Management folder, we have a conflicting permission situation.

Permission conflicts can and frequently do occur because of permissions inheritance through a group hierarchy, or through an object hierarchy. Permission conflicts usually occurs in the following situations:

- A user is a direct member of two groups, at least one of which directly grants the user a permission on an object, and at least one of the other groups, which effectively (directly) denies the user that permission on that object.

- The user might be in more than two groups, so there can be more than one conflicting grant and/or deny for the same permission.

- The groups can be organized in a hierarchical structure and conflicting direct permissions can originate from any of the groups in that hierarchy.

- The object for which the permission is being evaluated is in a hierarchical structure and inherits permissions from one or more parent objects (for example, folders).

- Two or more ACTs are applied to the object itself, or to any parent of the object, where one grants and the other denies a permission on the same object.

If you follow this rule and only grant access to explicit groups, permission conflicts can be avoided. Here are some additional tips to keep in mind when designing security models:

- When there is a permission conflict, to figure out whether SAS will grant a permission on an object for a user or deny it, you must know about and consider each grant or deny of that permission, which could affect the object in question and determine which of them takes precedence.

- You must consider the group hierarchy, which allows membership of multiple groups directly, and multiple membership paths from multiple parent groups.

- You must consider the entire object hierarchy.

- You must consider that ACEs take precedence over ACTs, if applied at the same level. ACTs and ACEs can be applied for multiple groups of which the user is a member. At the same level means in the object inheritance path and the same level in the identity hierarchy.

Paul Homes provided some good example scenarios for situations when applied to different levels.

Example 1: For a child folder, an ACE on the parent folder that denies WriteMetadata to SASUSERS, will be overridden by an ACT on the child folder that grants WriteMetadata to PUBLIC.

Example 2: On a single folder, an ACE that denies ReadMetadata to PUBLIC, will be overridden by an ACT on the same folder that grants ReadMetadata to SASUSERS.

At this point, you are probably asking yourself: WHY ME?!

Stay with me here, it does make sense. Whenever you have doubts, and whenever you are unsure how this permission matter works, the following figure illustrates the evaluation process that determines whether a restricted user (here called Joe) has a particular permission for a particular item (see Figure 6.7 – resource: https://support.sas.com/documentation/cdl/en/bisecag/61133/HTML/default/viewer.htm#a002 977119.htm).

Figure 6.7: Authorization decision flowchart

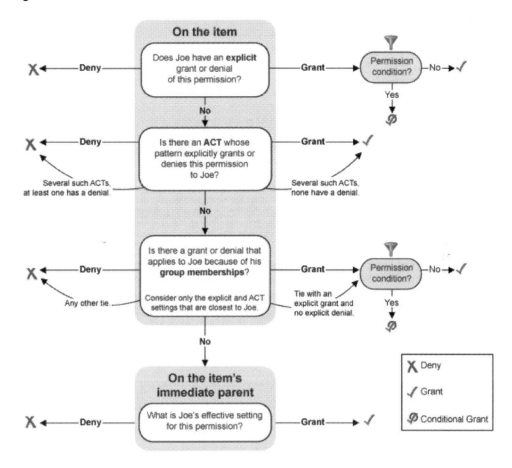

SAS provides authorization batch tools, that not only let you assign permissions or create ACTs, but you can use it to list the permissions your users have and where they belong to. (See the Appendix for the Batch Tool SAS documentation).

The rules SAS follows to determine how the conflicting permissions should be resolved are clearly defined but are complex. It can be exceptionally difficult for an administrator to follow. Few experienced SAS administrators understand the rules well enough to correctly predict whether the grant or deny will 'win' in even simple scenarios.

If you follow Rule 3 (ACTs using explicit groups (not PUBLIC or SASUSERS)), the effective permissions that a user has on an object are much easier to understand.

Simply look up the object hierarchy to determine the level nearest to the object at which PUBLIC and/or SASUSERS are denied a permission. The user's permissions are the sum of any permissions granted by other ACTs at that level of the hierarchy or below.

Rule 3 is one of the more difficult to comply with. It can be very tempting to check a deny check box in an ACT, or worse, in breach of Rule 1, check a deny check box in the

Authorization tab of an object or folder, to compensate for a group having unwanted access to a specific resource. But if you break this rule, you will sooner or later get a bad admin headache.

If you feel dizzy right about now, I understand, but please don't give up. You can do this! If I can, you can! The human brain has billions of neurons, each neuron is connected to thousand other neurons. That is what I call a complex relationship network. Compared to that, what is a little grant and deny.

Rule 4: Where Necessary, Apply ACTs to Deny Access to PUBLIC/SASUSERS, in Combination with ACTs to Grant a Reduced set of Permissions to Explicit Groups

This rule covers situations where you need to reduce or remove the access one or more groups have, to a metadata object (such as a folder) and its children. Only create permissions for a folder like this when there is no sensible alternative!

To reduce or remove access to an object (such as folder) for groups which would otherwise inherit broader access than you want them to have, apply the following:

- **PUBLIC and SASUSERS Denied ACT** (as a reminder, we created this ACT earlier in this chapter in the "creating custom ACTs" section.
- **SAS Administrator Settings ACT** (grant)
- Select **custom ACTs** to grant permissions for select groups

All users are members of the implicit group PUBLIC. Authenticated users with a metadata identity are also members of the implicit group SASUSERS, and probably belong to at least one explicit group (i.e. any group other than SASUSERS or PUBLIC).

If the existing ACTs featuring these groups are too permissive, create a new ACT which grants only the permissions that you want, and apply the new ACT to the object.

This rule does not conflict with Rule 3, because Rule 3 prohibits denying permissions to members of an *explicit* group, but in Rule 4 we apply ACTs which deny access to *implicit* groups only.

Explanation: This rule defines how you should restrict access to metadata objects in your folder or object hierarchy. It allows you to grant access to a more limited group or set of groups, and 'hide' and "protect" the metadata object and its child objects from all other groups.

To explain this rule, let's consider a permission such as ReadMetadata (RM), granted or denied for an object such as a metadata folder. The rule applies in exactly the same way to any permission on any object, but we will use this example because it is simple and easy to follow.

In this example, suppose that two groups, *group A* and *group B*, have inherited (gray) a grant of RM on the folder, but we only want *group A to have RM*, and we want *RM to be denied for group B.* We have a *Group A ACT* which *grants RM* to *Group A.* There is also a *Group B ACT* which *grants RM* to *Group B,* see Figure 6.8 below.

Figure 6.8: A folder intended for Group A only is beneath a parent folder that is accessible (i.e. it has Read Metadata permission granted) to Group B as well as to Group A

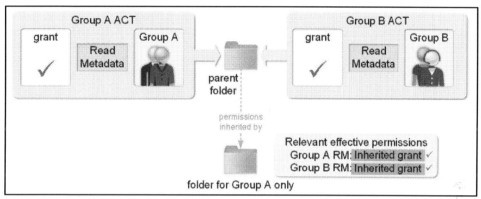

But we do not wish Group B to have ReadMetadata permission on 'folder for Group A only'. The simplest way to prevent Group B from reading the content of that folder would be to explicitly deny Group B ReadMetadata on that folder. But doing that would break two of our golden rules:

- Rule 1: Only use ACTs, never ACEs
- Rule 3: ACTs only grant access to explicit groups, never deny

So, we will solve this problem using an ACT. And we won't create or use an ACT which denies ReadMetadata (or any other permission) to Group B.

Solution: The correct way to meet the requirement to effectively deny Group B access to the '*folder for Group A only*', requires a *PUBLIC and SASUSERS Denied ACT* and a *SAS Administrator Settings ACT.* The figure below only shows the ReadMetadata grants in these ACTs, to avoid the figure becoming unnecessarily complicated. Many other permissions besides ReadMetadata are set in the complete definitions of these two ACTs.

Figure 6.9: Partial representations of a PUBLIC and SASUSERS Denied ACT, and a SAS Administrator Settings ACT, showing only the Read Metadata permissions that they deny and grant.

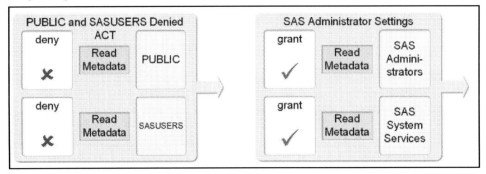

As seen in Figure 6.9, you should also apply the SAS Administrator Settings ACT wherever you apply the PUBLIC and SASUSERS Denied ACT.

Rule 1 says we must not explicitly apply an ACE on this folder to deny ReadMetadata for group B.

Rule 3 says we must not deny ReadMetadata to group B in an ACT and apply that ACT to the folder.

Instead, to remove the inherited ReadMetadata permission for group B, leaving it intact for group A, we apply:

- The **PUBLIC and SASUSERS Denied ACT**. This, on its own, denies ALL permissions for ALL users. Hint: do not apply this on its own! If you do, only an Unrestricted User will be able to see the object and its children!

- The **SAS Administrator Settings ACT.** This grants back the necessary minimum permissions SAS Administrators should have on all objects, and grants ReadMetadata to SAS System Services which requires RM on every object.

- By implementing the above, the conflict between SASUSERS and PUBLIC denied and granting back permission for SAS Administrators and SAS System Services is safely resolved in favor of the grants from the SAS Administrator Settings ACT. The SAS Administrators group within the ACT is an *explicit* group, PUBLIC and SASUSERS are *implicit* groups. An explicit group always takes precedence because the SAS Administrators group is closer to the user in his or her *identity hierarchy* than the implicit groups. Even if you apply both of these ACTs on the object, such as a folder, with a grant and deny on that object, in this case, the grant as the setting for the group closer to the user identity hierarchy takes precedence: because SAS Administrators is an explicit group, their permissions do take precedence.

Going back to the example for Group A and Group B: the **Group A ACT** which grants ReadMetadata (amongst other permissions) to Group A. Again, the conflict between the grant in this ACT and the deny in the **PUBLIC SASUSERS Denied ACT** is resolved in favor of the grant for members of Group A in this ACT, because an explicit group (Group A) is closer to the user in his identity hierarchy than an implicit group (SASUSERS or PUBLIC).

Figure 6.10: Three more ACTs (highlighted in orange) have been applied to 'folder for Group A only', with the result that Group A still has access to that folder, Group B does not, and none of the golden rules of security model design have been broken.

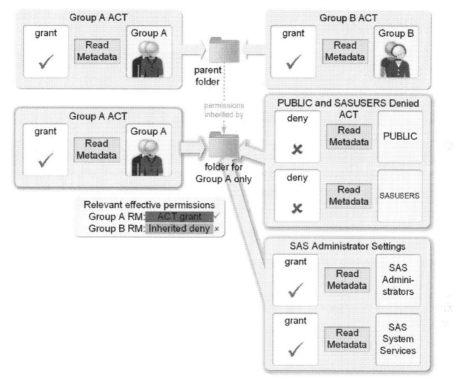

This leaves the folder accessible by SAS Administrators, SAS System Services and Group A as intended, but inaccessible (ReadMetadata is denied) for members of Group B and any other group that might be created in the future (unless it is a nested group for Group A or specifically granted), as intended.

Of course, in this example, in addition to the PUBLIC and SASUSERS Denied ACT and the SAS Administrators ACT which effectively set the permissions on a folder back to a minimum, we only added the Group A ACT back to 're-grant' access to the folder to that group. In real customer SAS deployments, there can be more than one group which needs to be 're-granted' access when you 'start again' by applying the PUBLIC and SASUSERS Denied ACT and the SAS Administrators ACT. You can have to apply several additional ACTs to the same folder to restore the desired permissions.

As you can see, the logic for determining effective permissions on an object for a user is somewhat complex. Follow rule 4 to avoid having to resolve the complex inheritance and precedence logic in your head to determine who wins in the event of conflicting grant and deny permissions effective on an object for a particular user! Rule 4 allows you to deny access to a folder, without breaking rules 1 and 3, and while keeping the logic simple and easy to follow.

It is extremely important to understand the effect of implicit and explicit:

- Direct Access Controls (ACEs) on one and the same object, with a grant and a deny for one person themselves and not any group they are member of, the deny will take precedence (this is just to show the net effect. Do not use ACEs!)

- Two custom groups are both considered explicit. If applied on the same object, such as a folder, both ACTs including a same direct user, one ACT granting the other denying, the deny takes precedence.

- A direct/custom ACT with granted permission and a *PUBLIC and SASUSERS denied ACT* (implicit groups) on the same object, such as a folder, the explicit group takes precedence, meaning, here, the grant takes precedence.

- In the object hierarchy, the permissions are checked bottom up, meaning, the "lowest" child's object permissions are evaluated first. If inherited without any explicit permissions applied, the parent object is checked to see whether there are explicit permissions, and so forth.

The following list summarizes rule 4:

- ACTs should be defined by denying permissions to the broadest identity level possible and granting permissions more precisely to the groups that require access.

- Implement by denying PUBLIC or SASUSERS then granting permissions selectively to groups.

- Avoids potential permission conflicts and unintended effective permissions caused by user error.

- Don't forget to grant back permissions to privileged identities.

Rule 5: Always Apply the SAS Administrators ACT when PUBLIC and SASUSERS Are Denied Access

Apply this rule in conjunction with Rule 4.

Always apply both the *SAS Administrators ACT* and the *PUBLIC and SASUSERS Denied ACT* together.

Explanation: While the SAS internal, unrestricted admin user - sasadm@saspw -is not subject to metadata permissions, all other users including members of the SAS Administrators group are. If you deny access to an object and its children to PUBLIC and SASUSERS you must make sure to always apply both the *SAS Administrators ACT* and the *PUBLIC and SASUSERS Denied ACT* together.

Rule 6: Design Your Security Model First and Implement It Early

As mentioned at the beginning of the best practices, planning is everything. Please do not take this lightly. Design an outline structure of your security model, with examples of detailed structural elements that you will repeat per team, project, data topic, business unit etc., early in the life of a SAS deployment.

Document your design clearly, in enough detail that someone else can understand it and implement it. Be thoughtful, other administrators might need this information as well. Store the document on a shared drive, OneDrive – whatever options you have in your company that allow for safe sharing amongst SAS administrators – and maybe even IT in cases where file system security might be brought in!

Be prepared to change the names of objects in your security model occasionally but avoid major redesigns in a live system.

Explanation: A security model implemented in a haphazard way without a clear design and without good design documentation is likely to contain numerous design errors and is likely to be implemented badly. Security models can appear simple but are usually complicated. You must make a design and follow that design closely in your implementation of the security model.

Ninety percent of the effort involved in creating a robust, maintainable security model is the design and the documentation. In comparison, implementation of the model is very easy. **Do not be tempted to skip the design and go straight to the implementation work.**

The downside of designing your security model early is that the names of groups, and their associated ACTs and folders chosen early in the life of a SAS deployment are often found to be inadequate as the use of the SAS deployment matures.

A group which is named "Developers," intended to represent any user performing any type of development, can need to be changed when it later becomes clear that you need "SAS Demand Intelligence Developers" and a new group "VA Report Developers," with corresponding new ACTs and folders. Your design should take into account that you might have to change the names of some objects in the security model over time, to better reflect what they now are. Minor changes, such as to object names (groups, ACTs, folders) can usually be managed without too much impact.

Some ongoing change in your wider security model design over time is unavoidable as the organizational structures evolve. However, it is *exceptionally disruptive* to users for major design changes to the security model to be made while the application content that those users work with is in development. It is *even worse* once the deployment is in live production use. Implementing the security model early in the life cycle of the SAS deployment will minimize this disruption.

Rule 7: Apply ACTs to Folders where Possible

Where possible, apply ACTs to metadata folders, rather than to objects. Only where that is not possible because the object is not in a metadata folder, you can apply ACTs to an object directly. It is a best practice to apply ACTs as high up in the folder hierarchy as possible.

Explanation: For example, to secure a library, put the metadata library definition in a metadata folder, and apply the necessary ACTs to that folder. As another example, if tables should have the same permissions as their parent library, put those tables in the same folder as the library. But when a table requires different permissions to its parent library, put it in another folder (for example, a subfolder of the folder containing the library), and apply ACTs to that folder to set the required permissions for the table.

Some objects which must be secured are not in the metadata folder tree. To set permissions on those objects and prevent them from being modified by users who should not be able to modify them, it is necessary to apply ACTs to the objects directly. Examples for object types for which this applies include ACTs themselves, application server Contexts such as SASApp and SASMeta, metadata server and logical server definitions, spawners etc.

Rule 8: Name Security Model Objects Clearly and Simply

Groups should be named to clearly indicate what they are. ACTs should be named for the single group that they feature, where possible. Naming your groups A, B, C and your ACTs Aa Bb Cc would certainly not make sense.

Explanation: Groups in an LDAP Provider such as Active Directory should be named in a way which satisfies the corporate naming convention for LDAP groups, while also indicating that the group is associated with a specific SAS deployment, tenant and or project. Good elements to include in the group name are as follows:

- "**SAS**" (to distinguish the group from Active Directory groups which have nothing to do with SAS).

- **The name of the whole SAS ecosystem** if the customer has more than one (for example, Marketing, Drug Development, Credit Risk, Pensions, Polling Data, Aerospace, Shipping) – a large SAS customer can have multiple SAS "applications" built on entirely separate sets of hardware and managed essentially separately from each other, yet they can share a common corporate LDAP service. You should omit this element if the customer has only one SAS ecosystem or environment.

- If there are multiple SAS deployments in one ecosystem, **the name of the SAS deployment** within in its ecosystem (such as Dev, Test or Prod). In the LDAP service, there will be groups with otherwise identical names, one set for each of the SAS deployments in the customer's ecosystem (Dev, Test and Prod). Having the name of the SAS deployment as one part of the group name helps the SAS and LDAP administrators distinguish between the groups belonging to for each separate SAS deployment, in the directory service.

- If relevant, **the name of the tenant** organization and/or project within the ecosystem, when a single SAS deployment or ecosystem is used by several companies, divisions, departments, teams or projects.

- The part of the group name which indicates **what its members do** in the SAS deployment, for example, DI Developers, VA Report Designers etc.

In an organization with many SAS ecosystems, each having multiple tenants, and each tenant having multiple projects, the names of groups in Active Directory can be long and complex. **Dynamic groups** (i.e. groups which are synchronized into SAS metadata from an

LDAP service provider) should have names which match the name in that LDAP service provider as closely as possible. For example: *Example Active Directory Group Name*, also name of corresponding dynamic group in SAS metadata. Keeping the names the same or very similar makes it easier for administrators to understand which groups correspond to each other later. One element you can consider removing from group names as you synchronize them with SAS metadata is the part which identifies the deployment within the ecosystem (for example, Dev, Test or Prod). If you choose to implement shadow groups (static groups which mirror your dynamic groups), you can keep the deployment name element in the dynamic group name. If you will use dynamic groups directly in ACTs, you should remove the "SAS deployment name" (Dev/Test/Prod) element from the SAS metadata group name, so that your ACTs contain groups with the same name in each SAS deployment in your ecosystem. This is helpful, for example, when importing and exporting standard ACTs across environments,

If the corporate naming convention does not allow LDAP groups to be named in this manner, define the best names that you are able to in the LDAP directory service, and create a lookup table and a step in your user and group synchronization program, to associate each dynamic group with its corresponding static group. That lookup table is then the reference defining which groups correspond to each other.

Static groups in SAS metadata (i.e. groups which are NOT synchronized from an LDAP service provider) should have names which omit most of the elements above, concentrating on the part of the group name which indicates what its members do in this specific SAS deployment, for example, DI Developers, VA Report Designers etc. One SAS deployment does not usually need to have objects in it whose names reference other SAS deployments, or even hint that other SAS deployments can exist. For example, it is not necessary for DI Developers in a Development environment to be labeled "Dev DI Developers." "DI Developers" is better.

How in the world do I know whether what I implemented is good? Look at your security testing options.

The complete article for the rules above can be found in the Appendix: https://communities.sas.com/t5/SAS-Communities-Library/Golden-Rules-for-Security-Model-Design/ta-p/373542

Security Testing Options

As I mentioned above, implementing best practices is important in having a more secure environment, so how do you know whether your environment is secure if you don't test it? Worry no more. Let me introduce you to some great security testing options available. The first option I would like to talk about is SAS Environment Manager. After that, I will introduce you to a SAS partner, Metacoda, who provide tools to help keep your SAS platform secure.

SAS Environment Manager

I recommend that you use SAS Environment Manager for reporting and auditing on your metadata security. Keeping track of your users and permissions, you can use the SAS

Environment Manager *Report Center. (See Chapter 3 for information on SAS Environment Manager.)* In the following screenshots that you can see the users, groups, permissions activity related reports.

In SAS Environment Manager, expand the *Analyze* menu, choose *Report Center*. The reports under *Metadata Inventory* and *Audit Reports* are especially helpful. (See following screenshots 6.11 and 6.12.)

Figure 6.11: Metadata Inventory Reports

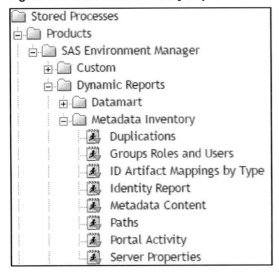

Figure 6.12: Audit Reports

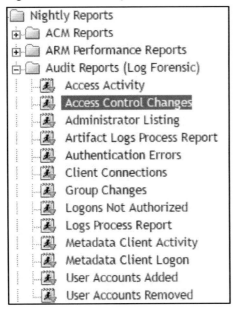

Note: If you get a note that the Report Center is not initialized when you choose *Analyze, Report Center*, please follow the instructions in the documentation SAS Environment Manager Extended Monitoring Steps, available at: http://support.sas.com/documentation/cdl/en/evug/69029/HTML/default/viewer.htm#p0h 7p9v8da676jn13vcjbl21rd05.htm

Metacoda Plugins

Metacoda offers security plugins that are implemented into the SAS Management Console. Metacoda software helps SAS platform administrators to regularly manage, review, troubleshoot, document, test and audit their SAS platform installation with confidence. These plugins can help with best practice testing. In other words, how well the implementation aligns with best practices such as the well-known Golden Rules. Implementation testing, which gives the effective result of the implementation, is also possible with the Metacoda tools. Check it out: https://www.metacoda.com/en/products/security-plug-ins/

Maintenance and Housekeeping

Maintaining and administering is an important part of security. What you implement must be monitored, and probably fine-tuned over time. Please keep the following in mind:

- Users come and go, or change teams, projects, or departments, and the teams, projects, departments, and the data, jobs, reports and other work products in use on the SAS system evolve.

- No security model implementation is ever perfect, and maintenance activity can introduce errors which were not there previously. Errors or shortcomings present in the model should be actively addressed over time. Please do not take this lightly.

- When users approach you due to authorization errors, please do not address this by just opening up the permissions, meaning by granting any permission just so the users can work. Situations like that could be indications that your security model must be adjusted. Or, maybe a user tries to access data they are not supposed to access. Review your security model to see whether it is still appropriate or whether it might need some adjustment. Test it regularly to make sure your environment is still protected appropriately. It is of the utmost important that you try to avoid waiting until users approach you. Always make sure, test and verify that user/groups have grants where they are supposed to and denies where it is important they do not have access to. You will most likely not be approached if users have too much access. For that reason it is important to always keep an eye on the security implementation.

- The best scenario of course would be if you'd have a test environment in which you could mimic users, groups, folders, and permissions. etc. This would allow you to test and "play." You would not have to re-create everything but could use the export and import features in SAS Management Console. See Promoting Specific Object Types https://go.documentation.sas.com/?cdcId=bicdc&cdcVersion=9.4&docsetId=bisag& docsetTarget=n1f9181cn1d545n1odu6hkrrcee4.htm&locale=en for details. If you want to test client access to see whether users/groups permissions work, promotion requires that your test environment has the same OS accounts that you used on your production environment. If you are an admin who won the "I have more machines than I can count available" jackpot, you could even consider an admin-only environment.

- Whenever you do make changes, please run a SAS backup. See the next chapter for details.

These contributions and documented resources for best practice are from a paper Cecily and Johannes wrote, called "Best Practice Implementation of SAS Metadata Security at Customer Sites in Denmark": http://support.sas.com/resources/papers/proceedings11/376-2011.pdf.

More resources can be found in the Appendix.

Summary

There is a lot to say about security, and even though there is a lot to learn, and even though there are so many things to pay attention to when implementing security, just focus on the best practice provided in this chapter. Understand permission inheritance and how permissions on different levels can conflict with each other. Become familiar with Access Control Templates. And most importantly: make sure you have a good plan and strategy in mind before implementing security. Keep in mind that implementing security is not a one-time matter. It must be maintained and administered. Implement security wisely. Remember:

"Knowledge is knowing that a tomato is a fruit. Wisdom is not putting it into a fruit salad."
Unknown

Chapter 7: Backup and Restore: Should Have, Could Have, Would Have ... Famous Last Words

Introduction

If your backup plan objective time is "whenever," we must talk!

Backup strategies are of the UTMOST importance. You must have a good backup strategy in place. Just as important as the backup is, you must also have a very well-rehearsed restore/recovery procedure in place to avoid disaster. A restore/recovery rehearsal validates that the backups are usable and complete, and it also provides a practice so that when the time comes to do it for real it can be done efficiently to get the business going again as soon as possible.

Do you know how often we get frantic calls at SAS because someone cannot access their data anymore due to corruption? When asked for a backup to perform a restore, customers often have a backup from 6-month, x month, ago or do not have a backup at all. Or if they do have backups that are taken daily, they did not consider that the SAS deployment needs to be backed up as well. These situations are pretty catastrophic. I have seen every worst-case scenario – months' worth of work lost (not even mentioning the money lost) and situations where hundreds of users were unable to work because the SAS environment became corrupted. I am not painting a dark picture to convince you – this is reality.

So, in this chapter, we are going to cover backups in SAS. Print this chapter, frame it and hang it on your wall. I am even considering recording an audio book that admins can listen to on their way to work. Seriously, it is that important.

If you ever listened in to one of my admin Webexes, or if we talked on the phone about admin tasks, you know how much I like to stress this topic.

Backup, Backup and Backup Again

A common question customers ask is: what's all the fuss about SAS backup? I am running file system backups, is that not enough? The simple answer is: NO, it is not. Absolutely and utterly not!

As always in life, there are unforeseen events and, unless you have a crystal ball to foresee the future, you might want to prepare yourself. Think about it: do you have car insurance? Insurance for your house?

If you don't backup your SAS environment, you will lose data should a restore become necessary. There is no way back.

Why File System Backups are Not Enough

The file system backup that runs – hopefully – daily must be synchronized with SAS. There are many different SAS components which are working asynchronously. A successful SAS backup involves backing up the state of each of these components, including how they relate to one another. A file system backup takes file snapshots at a specified point in time, regardless of the state of the SAS components.

When we talk about backing up your SAS environment, it's about making sure that you take care of your assets. It is about having backups including these assets, safely stored away.

Let's revisit the SAS architecture quickly to give you a picture of what must be backed up. Whether you are on a single machine or a multi machine environment, your SAS architecture consists of 3-plus 1 tiers (plus 1 being the data tier, which too has to be considered in the backup strategy as it is used within SAS!)

As a reminder of the tiers, check out Table 7.1.

Table 7.1: SAS Architecture

Data Tier	SAS Server Tier	Middle Tier	SAS Client Tier
SAS Data Sets	SAS Metadata Server	SAS Web Server	Desktop Clients: SAS Add-In for Microsoft Office
OLAP Cubes	SAS Workspace Server		
		SAS Web Application Server	
SAS Scalable Performance Data Server (SPDS)	SAS Pooled Workspace Server		SAS Data Integration Studio
	SAS OLAP Server	SAS Web Infrastructure Platform	SAS Enterprise Miner
SAS Web Infrastructure Platform Data Server	SAS Stored Process Server	SAS Content Server and other infrastructure applications and service	SAS Forecast Studio

Data Tier	SAS Server Tier	Middle Tier	SAS Client Tier
	These servers are running SAS processes for distributed clients		
Third-Party Data Sources (such as Oracle, Teradata etc.)		Web Clients: (run in an instance of the SAS Web Application Server). The SAS web clients are:	SAS Enterprise Guide
			SAS Information Map Studio
Hadoop		SAS Web Report Studio	
			SAS Management Console
Enterprise Resource Planning (ERP) Systems		SAS Information Delivery Portal	
			SAS Model Manager
		SAS BI Portlets	
			SAS OLAP Cube Studio
		SAS BI Dashboard	
		SAS Help Viewer for the Web	SAS Workflow Studio
		Other SAS Web Applications and Solutions	JMP
			Other SAS analytics products and solution
		SAS Environment Manager	
			Web Browser to surface web Applications
			Mobile Devices, if applicable, to view certain type of reports.

What Must be Backed Up in SAS?

When we talk about backing up your assets or your SAS content, we want to make sure the following is included in the backups:

- All metadata repositories (Foundation and any custom or project repositories that you might have created).

- Your SAS Content Server.

- Databases that are used by the SAS Web Infrastructure Platform Data server (such as Postgres, for example, which is used for SAS Environment Manager).

- Server configuration files and installation files (Complete contents of the `SAS-configuration-directory/Levn` directory).

- Physical content in files and databases.
- Reference locations for symbolic links.
- Batch server components.
- SASHOME needs to be included in the file system backup.

Depending on which of the backup tools you use, or a combination of the backup tools, additional steps might have to be taken. Often, IT is responsible for backups, and often, it turns out that the SAS content and its configuration directories are not included. As a first step, talk to your IT department, System admins – whoever is responsible for running backups in your company. Ask them if they run daily backups. If they don't and ask why they should, tell them "because SAS told me so." If they do not run daily backups, maybe you can find out why, and make suggestions as to why it is so important.

It is also important to talk to your system admins about the SAS environment, the data that you are using, and the locations where the data might be outputted to. Inform them where the data your users are using is located. Maybe take them through a high-level overview of the SAS architecture so that they are aware of the SAS content and configuration files. Share with them when your users are the most active, and whether there are jobs running at night at certain times. Verify that you as the admin have all the permissions needed to run ad hoc SAS backups and – if it would become necessary – can restore from backup. Another good reason why you should talk to your system admins is that you can explain to them what **not** to back up. A good example is SAS work/util, which might save them lots of backup storage space.

Often, it seems as if systems admins, database admins, and SAS admins are somewhat siloed. It is important that you communicate and that all backups are in-sync.

Important: A SAS Backup does NOT replace a file system/OS or third-party backup!

Backup and Restore Tools

The following is a summary of the backup facilities that are available to you in SAS 9.4. I won't go into much functionality detail as it is very well documented, but I would like to give a few pointers for each of the different options, and briefly compare them at the end.
Metadata Backup Facility

The Metadata Backup Facility existed prior to SAS 9.4. This backup facility provides the following:

1. An automatic nightly backup. By default, it is scheduled to run each night at 1am, except Sundays.
2. A reorganization option which removes unclaimed disk space of metadata objects that have been deleted.
3. Ad Hoc backup option. This is very useful for situations when you want to back up your metadata "on the fly", outside of the regular scheduled backup hour. Use it when you are going to make any changes to your environment, for example, make a major change to a configuration file.

4.   Recovery facility which is roll-forward.
5.   Backup history.

In addition to the automatic backup the facility takes, you can run ad hoc backups, use batch tools, or the SAS Deployment Backup and Recovery Tool (short DBRT).

> **Note:** You can run ad hoc backups at any time without effecting your users. The SAS backup runs in a separate thread, which means, the metadata server remains online even as the backup runs. The only exception is when you select to re-org. For a reorganization, the metadata server will be paused
>
> Restores provide a roll-forward process, so you can restore to a specific point in time.
>
> Please note: If you chose the Reorganize column in your backup, the SAS Metadata Server is placed in read-only mode, and requests to update the metadata are rejected until the reorganization is complete.

If you are interested in how a roll-forward process is managed, take a look at Journal Files. A journal file is just that: a journal in which you write all the things that are important to you (until your little brother gets a hand on it and sells it to the highest bidder).

A link for documentation about how to change the backup schedule can be found in the Appendix.

> **Note**: When you change the scheduling times for the *Metadata Backup Facility* in SAS Management Console and the schedule time in the *Backup Manager* in SAS Environment Manager, you must make sure that times do not overlap. Otherwise, the backups will interfere with each other. This is also true in cases where you schedule SAS backups via OS commands. Make sure that SAS backups run in different time windows.

Backups are retained for 7 days. That means, the Monday backup overwrites the backup taken exactly a week ago. Should a backup fail, SAS does not delete this backup and keeps it aside of the 7-day policy.

Let's look at the metadata backup facility via SAS Management Console. You can access the backup and restore facility via SAS Management Console, Metadata Manager plug-in, as shown in Figure 7.1.

Figure 7.1: Metadata Manager Plug-in

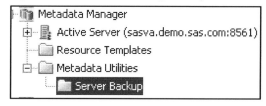

The first thing you will see is your backup history, as shown in Figure 7.2.

Figure 7.2: Backup History

Status	Type	Date Created
✓	Backup	Nov 14, 2018 7:42:25 PM
✓	Backup	Nov 14, 2018 4:02:01 PM
✓	Backup	Nov 14, 2018 1:00:00 AM
✓	Backup	Nov 13, 2018 10:41:13 PM
✓	Backup	Nov 12, 2018 1:00:00 AM
✓	Backup	Nov 10, 2018 1:00:00 AM
⚠	Backup	Nov 7, 2018 1:00:00 AM
⚠	Backup	Nov 5, 2018 1:00:00 AM
⚠	Backup	Nov 3, 2018 10:00:33 PM
⚠	Backup	Nov 3, 2018 1:00:00 AM

The green status icon indicates successful backups that are available for restore. The yellow exclamation mark shows the backups that have been deleted based on the 7-day retention policy. If you right-click on a green-checked backup – an active one – look at the Properties. It will show you details about the backup. If you look at the properties of an archived backup, you still can see the properties, but it shows as offline as it was deleted due to the 7-days policy.

Backups are written to:
SAS-configuration-directory/Lev1/SASMeta/MetadataServer/Backups

> **Best Practice:** Consider saving and storing your SAS backups files to a different machine or a different disk, to keep the actual SAS environment and backup files separate from each other. If you run a clustered metadata server environment, a shared location (vault) is required.

- You can specify any network location that is accessible from the metadata server. If you want to write the backup files to a path that is remote to the metadata server, then specify a UNC path (for example, **\\D12345\SASBackup**).
- If your metadata server is installed on a Windows host, do not specify a mapped drive.
- Make sure that the directory is specified as a shared directory and that the process owner for the metadata server has been granted full access.
- Be sure to include the directory in your regular system backups.

Who is Running the Backup?

To run a backup, the user has to be an unrestricted admin user (sasadm@saspw), a member of the SAS Administrators group, or a user who owns the capability to operate the metadata server. To access all the other backup options in SAS Management Console, you can do so by right-clicking on the *Server Backup*, as shown in Figure 7.3.

Figure 7.3: Server Backup

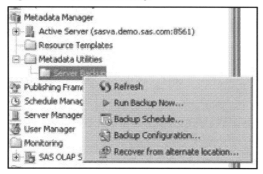

Batch Tools

Backup

Instead of running an ad hoc backup from within SAS Management Console, you can run ad hoc backups in batch as well. The result is the same, and what is happening behind the scenes is the same. Same schedule, same file location. The backup batch tools could be used, as one example, if you want to trigger the backup as part of a custom system backup script.

To run an ad hoc backup via command line:

Go to `SAS-configuration-directory/Lev1/SASMeta/MetadataServer` and run the following command:

Windows: **MetadataServer backup**

UNIX: **MetadataServer.sh backup**

This executes a program called *backupServer.sas*

You can edit the file to take a look at it – but, please do not change it.

> **Note:** If you edit *backupServer.sas*, you will notice the following entry:
>
> `'sas-config-dir\Lev1\SASMeta\MetadataServer\metaparms.sas'`
>
> The *metaparms* configuration file is located in the same location as the *backupServer.sas*. The file includes the connection information to the metadata server for the unrestricted user:
> ```
> options metaserver='machine_name'
> metaport=8561
> metaprotocol='bridge'
> metauser='sasadm@saspw'
> metapass='{sas002}1D57933958C580064BD3DCA81A33DFB2'
> metarepository='Foundation'
> metaconnect='NONE'
> ;
> ```

As you can see, the file includes sensitive information. For that reason, please be sure to protect this file so that only administrators can access it. Overview of operating system protection for SAS configuration files can be found in the Appendix. When you run an ad hoc backup using the backup batch tools, the backup information will appear in the backup history of SAS Management Console. You cannot use the Reorganize option when using this method.

Restore

A right-click on a green-checked backup also provides you the option to restore, as shown in figure 7.4.

Figure 7.4: Recovering from a Metadata Backup

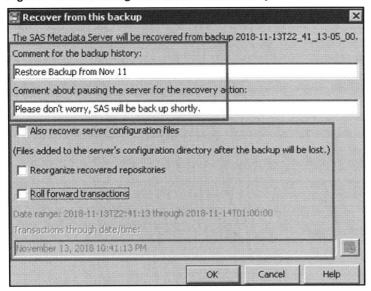

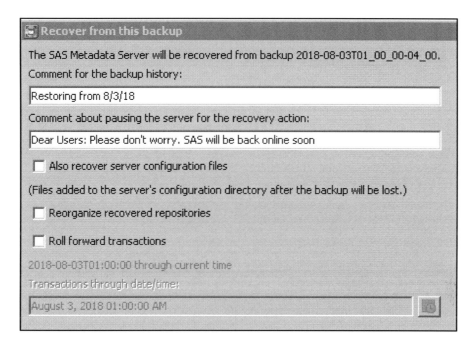

The restore window lets you document why you must restore, and you can add a note that will be sent to your users. A pop-up window will appear for them informing them. You then can choose if configuration files should be recovered as well, whether a reorganization should run once its restored, and you can enable a roll-forward option to choose a date.

> **Note**: Configuration files should only be restored if really necessary. Reasons for restoring configuration files are corrupted configuration files that cannot be corrected by editing. When you check the option to restore your configuration files, all files are going to be deleted and will be overwritten by the configuration files that were used on the day on which the backup you recover from, was taken. That means, any changes you might have made to the configuration files since then, will be lost.

You cannot restore from a backup that has been deleted (archived). If you attempt to do so, you will get the following error message: "Recover Error: A recover cannot be run because this backup is offline and not available".

More brainfood on this topic in the Appendix of this chapter.

Let's move on to the next option you have available to back up your SAS environment.

Operating System Commands

Backup

If you choose to use operating systems commands to backup the metadata, you can certainly do so. It is, however, imperative that you pause the metadata server before running a backup with system commands and then resume it. There are several ways to pause the server. The first way is via the SAS Management Console Server Manager plug-in – expand the metadata server, right-click on the lowest level, PAUSE. Another way is to use the scripts that are available in the metadata server directory: `sas-config-dir\Lev1\SASMeta\MetadataServer`. The file is called *pauseServer.sas*. Finally, you could use the *metaoperate* procedure.

Example of a PROC METAOPERATE to pause the metadata server to an offline state

```
proc metaoperate
      server="host-name"
      port=8561
      userid="user-ID"
      password="encoded-password"
      protocol=bridge
      action=pause
      noautopause;
run;
```

Example to resume the metadata server.

```
proc metaoperate
      server="host-name"
      port=8561
      userid="user-ID"
      password="encoded-password"
      protocol=bridge
      action=resume
      noautopause;
run;
```

The user that is specified in *user-ID* must be assigned to the **Metadata Server: Operation** role.

Link for further info – see Appendix.

Why is It So Important to Pause the Metadata Server?

The metadata server is an in-memory server, which means, a copy of the metadata (not the actual data!) your users access, is written to memory. It is kept there until the metadata server is paused and resumed, or stopped and restarted. The pause or stop is used to flush any very recent as-yet unwritten changes to disk and also to stop metadata server clients from doing any updates during the backup. That way the repository files can be backed-up without fear of them being partially modified during the backup and losing integrity. Having some files backed up before a change and some after would make the backup not usable Think of it as a puzzle: if you have a puzzle and you throw away some of the puzzle pieces, you won't be able to put the puzzle back together. This is the same concept.

Restore

Using the command line interface, you can restore content using the *restore* option.

It uses the Metadata Server Backup Facility as described above.

Promotion (Export and Import Wizards)

Backup

Using the promotion tools – as the Export and Import SAS Package Wizards are referred to – enables you to backup specific content. The wizards are also used to copy partial content between SAS environments. It is a great option when you move from one SAS version to another and don't want to use migration, or you might want to move content between dev, test and prod environments.

From a backup perspective, you can use the wizard to "pack up" objects in your SAS folders (SAS Management Console's Folders tab). An example of a situation where this might come in handy is when a user or a group has finished a big project and you want to explicitly stack it away or copy the content into a production environment.

You can run an export and import using batch commands as well. Running it in batch allows you to schedule package-based backups. For more information, check out the Appendix.

Restore

Using the Import Wizard, you can import the metadata content that you exported. The export creates a package file (. spk). When importing from an SPK file, associations must be considered.

Continuing with export and import, the export and import tools come into handy really when there is only very little content that you want to back up "in between". Please do NOT use this method solely because it might sound like the easiest one out of all backup and restore methods. Always consider that the Export and Import Wizards are **only** to be used if you want to save **partial** content **in addition** to your regular backup!

Next, let's talk about the backup tool that was newly introduced in SAS 9.4.

Deployment Backup and Recovery Tool (DBRT)

You can access the Deployment Backup and Recovery Tool via SAS Environment Manager or choose to use batch commands. SAS Environment Manager is accessed via web browser, using the following link: http://machinename.com:7080/ where "machinename" is the name of your middle tier machine. Port 7080 is the default port used during the SAS deployment.

If you are unsure whether the default port was used, or, what the exact link is, you can look at the instructions.html file. This file is stored at **SAS-config-dir/Lev1/Documents/**. The instructions.html file is created after your SAS environment has been installed and configured; it includes important information about your install and configuration, such as paths, ports used, links, default users created etc. It can generally be helpful to look up information about your SAS configuration.

The SAS DBRT is accessed via the *Administration* menu in SAS Environment Manager, *Backup Manager*. Looking at the options in SAS Environment Manager's *Administration* tab, you will notice some of the tasks that you can do in SAS Management Console are available here as well. You can manage folders and objects, servers, libraries, users, and metadata security and access controls

Backup

The SAS DBRT tool backs up the following content:

- SAS Metadata Server (everything under **sas-config-dir\Lev1\SASMeta\MetadataServer**).

- Databases managed by the SAS Web Infrastructure Platform Data Server, for example, Postgres. You can change the default if you would want to modify which database are to be backed up.

- SAS Content Server.

- Configuration directories:
  - **Data** directories and **SASEnvironment** directories for the SAS Metadata Server and SAS Application Server context (in **sas-config-dir\Lev1\SASMeta** and **sas-config-dir\Lev1\SASApp**.)
  - Directories for SAS Application Server components on the SAS server tier (**sas-config-dir \Lev1\ConnectSpawner**), except batch server components and the SAS Grid Server component.
  - Directories for each spawner used by the SAS Application Server component on the SAS server tier (example: **sas-config-dir \Lev1\ConnectSpawner**, **sas-config-dir\Lev1\ObjectSpawner**).

- Any additional custom directories (https://go.documentation.sas.com/?docsetId=bisag&docsetTarget=n0khpcet4rb0syn191i08w765cw1.htm&docsetVersion=9.4&locale=en#p19w36holp8xnun1d58ivstagzh1) you might have created under **SAS-configuration-directory/Levn**. It uses the metadata server backup facility that we described earlier.

Vault

The backup files are written to **SAS-configuration-directory/Lev1/Backup/Vault** on each machine, where they are kept for 30 days. This backup location is automatically created for you when you run your backup for the first time.

Instead of using the backup location on each individual machine, you have the option to create a central vault location. When you have a central vault location, the backup files on each individual machine are written to this central location. Creating a central vault location is a safety measure because you can specify a network location or directory that has all backed up content together.

Important: If you choose to create a central vault location on a network drive, you must make sure that the vault location is available and accessible at any time. SAS DBRT can only backup or restore if the specified location is available. Make sure you choose a vault directory that has enough disk space to store backup files for 30 days. Lastly, using a shared vault location is recommended in case a host machine goes down to avoid the loss of backup files.

Vault locations can be set up for homogeneous and heterogeneous environments. As promised, I won't mention that there is more to read up on in the Appendix of this chapter.

If you did not install and configure SAS 9.4 and you are not sure if a central vault location has been configured, there are two ways for you to find out:

- Go to the Backup Manager in SAS Environment Manager, under the Administration menu to look at the Backup Policy.
- Look at the policy configuration in batch, use **sas-display-backup-config**.

Aside from running backups or listing configuration settings, the sas-display-backup provides other good information about the backup settings.

In case troubleshooting would become necessary:

Log File

The log with information from the backup server is located at **sas-config-dir\Lev1\Backup** and is called **backupserver.log**
There is another log file that logs the communication between the SAS Deployment Agents and the Backup Server on each tier in your SAS deployment located here: **sas-config-dir\Lev1\Web\Logs\SASServer1_1** called **SASDeploymentBackup9.4.log.**

The name of the default SAS Web Application Server managing clients such as the SAS DBRT, SAS Environment Manager, SAS Web Report Studio is Ad SASServer1_1.

If you would like to enable debug logging, the first step to keep the original SASDeploymentBackup9.4.log is to rename the file.

Go to **sas-config-dir\Lev1\Web\Logs\SASServer1_1** and rename **SASDeploymentBackup9.4.log** to something like *oldSASDeploymentBackup9.4.*

The next steps in the process to enable debug logging are as follows:

Go to **sas-config\Lev1\Web\Common\LogConfig** and edit the file **SASDeploymentBackup-log4j.xml.**

Look for the following entry:

```
<category additivity="false" name="com.sas.svcs.backup">
        <priority value="WARN"/>
        <appender-ref ref="SAS_CONSOLE"/>
  <appender-ref ref="SAS_FILE"/>
```

Change the logging level to DEBUG

Note: Changing the logging level to DEBUG will create more detailed log files, and, consequently, bigger in size log files. Consider whether you want to increase the logging level only temporarily for troubleshooting, or if you want to keep the increased logging level.

If you look at the **`backupserver.log,`** look for the entry **`com.sas.svcs.backup.server.handler.LevconfigBackupHandler`** to see a list of the components that are included in the backup, as seen in Figure 7.5.

Figure 7.5: Log File Content

```
com.sas.svcs.backup.server.handler.LevconfigBackupHandler - Calling cmu to backup sas config directory
com.sas.svcs.backup.server.handler.LevconfigBackupHandler - Scanning for server directories to be backed up
com.sas.svcs.backup.server.handler.LevconfigBackupHandler - Folder added as Server directory : ConnectSpawner ,
com.sas.svcs.backup.server.handler.LevconfigBackupHandler - Folder added as Server directory : Data , folder : D:\o
com.sas.svcs.backup.server.handler.LevconfigBackupHandler - Folder added as Server directory : ObjectSpawner , fold
com.sas.svcs.backup.server.handler.LevconfigBackupHandler - Folder added as Server directory : SchedulingServer , f
com.sas.svcs.backup.server.handler.LevconfigBackupHandler - Folder added as Server directory : BatchServer , folder
com.sas.svcs.backup.server.handler.LevconfigBackupHandler - Folder added as Server directory : ConnectServer , fold
com.sas.svcs.backup.server.handler.LevconfigBackupHandler - Folder added as Server directory : OLAPServer , folder
com.sas.svcs.backup.server.handler.LevconfigBackupHandler - Folder added as Server directory : PooledWorkspaceServer
com.sas.svcs.backup.server.handler.LevconfigBackupHandler - Folder added as Server directory : StoredProcessServer ,
com.sas.svcs.backup.server.handler.LevconfigBackupHandler - Folder added as Server directory : WorkspaceServer , fo
com.sas.svcs.backup.server.handler.LevconfigBackupHandler - Folder added as Server directory : PooledWorkspaceServer
com.sas.svcs.backup.server.handler.LevconfigBackupHandler - Folder added as Server directory : WorkspaceServer , fo
com.sas.svcs.backup.server.handler.LevconfigBackupHandler - Folder added as Server directory : PooledWorkspaceServer
com.sas.svcs.backup.server.handler.LevconfigBackupHandler - Folder added as Server directory : WorkspaceServer , fo
```

> **Note:** At one-point, custom directories were created with the `sas-add-backup-customdir` command. This command is no longer available in SAS 9.4 M3 and later. You now create custom directories using **sas-update-backup-config.** You cannot add the entire SAS configuration directory (Lev*n*) as a custom directory. This is not supported. You can only add individual directories underneath Lev*n*.

> **Note:** If you are using symbolic links for any of the listed configuration directories, you must back them up with the file system backup. Symbolic links are not included in the SAS backups.

Views

The first view you have in DBRT is the *History* view. As Figure 7.6 shows, the history status is marked with a green check mark for successful backups, and the red circle indicates that the backups have been archived.

Figure 7.6: History view

Status	Backup ID	User ID	Size	Start Time
⊘	2018-11-19T14_05_57	sasadm	73.0 MB	Nov 19, 2018, 2:06:03 PM
⃠	2017-12-24T01_00_14	sasadm	67.7 MB	Dec 24, 2017, 1:00:20 AM

If there were any errors when the backup was taken, an alert email is sent to the user that was specified during the SAS installation.

On the left top corner of Backup Manager, you can switch from the *History* view to *Policy* or *Schedule*. The *Policy* option provides the same graph as the *Diagram* view. The *Schedule* option lets you modify the default schedule for backups. The difference between the *Policy* view and *View Diagram* is that *Policy* shows you what is generally backed up per default, while *View Diagram* shows what has actually been backed up, displaying a green check if the backup on the different machines was successful or a red marker if it failed as shown in Figure 7.7.

Figure 7.7: View Diagram

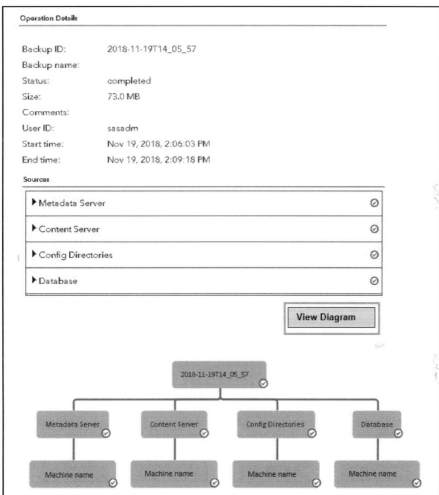

On the right bottom corner of this window you will find the *Start Backup* button for immediate, non-scheduled backups.

History

Using the sas-list-backups command, you can see the history of backups taken, along with information about whether each backup was successful or failed. You can also view the backup history via SAS Management Console, Metadata Manager plug-in, Metadata Utilities, Server Backup.

Restore

Just as you can restore in SAS Management Console, you can restore backups that have been taken via the Backup Manager in SAS Environment Manager. To do so, you would use the **execute sas-recover-offline** command.

Using this command restores everything that has been included in your backup at once. You can run the command from any machine in your environment, and it knows precisely where each component belongs.

> **Note:** To make sure you choose the correct backup to restore, be sure to run a **sas-list-backup**. This will provide you with a list of backups to choose from. Choose the most recent, successfully completed backup. Then run the **sas-display-backup** command to make sure that the backup that you chose does not show as **offline**. This would mean that the backup is past the 30-day rule and therefore expired. The sas-display-backup must list the components that are backed up, as **complete** – which means that the backup was completed successfully. It must show everything that is automatically backed up by the SAS DBRT.
>
> **Important:** If you - between the last backup and the actual restore - updated to a new SAS version, or, changed your host names using the *Update Host Name Reference* tool, you must make sure that you do not restore from a backup that was taken before that. Chances are that you will run into problems, and - worst case – cannot work with your environment. It is for that very reason why it is so imperative to take good backups before and immediately right after a major change has been made.

For details and further explanations on restoring using the restore command line interface, please take a close look at the documentation on performing a recovery using the Deployment Backup and Recovery Tool.

Depending on the SAS 9.4 maintenance release you have installed, some functionality can or cannot be available to you. You can look at "What's New in SAS 9.4" for the SAS platform, as it lists everything that is new based on maintenance releases. The version of SAS DBRT described in this chapter was available starting with SAS 9.4 Maintenance release 3 (M3).

> **Best Practice:** Backups that have been taken with the SAS DBRT, can be restored partially (only certain source types). However, it is recommended to retire restore from an entire backup.

A new interface to the SAS Backup and Recovery Tool is available from the Administration application in SAS Environment Manager. This new SAS Backup Manager interface makes scheduling regular backups and executing ad hoc backups extremely easy to do and greatly simplifies the life of a SAS administrator. For more information see the blog, Deleting old backups with SAS Backup Manager at blogs.sas.com.

Comparison of SAS Backup Tools

Table 7.2 compares SAS backup tools, what each one backs up and what the tool is used for.

Table 7.2: Comparison of SAS Backup Tools

Name of Backup Tool	What is backed up	What it is used for
SAS Metadata Server Backup Facility in SAS Management Console	All metadata content, configuration files	Ad Hoc backups Automatic nightly backup for all days of the week except Sunday. Nightly backups do not need any interaction Restore
Batch tools	All metadata content, configuration files	Ad Hoc backups OS scheduled, interactive backup Requires the metadata server to be paused and resumed Manual backup
Promotion (Export Wizard in SAS Management Console)	Partial content (Do not use Promotion as your general backup tool, but as an addition for situations where partial content has to be backup up.)	Backing up partial content in batch or interactively Ad Hoc backup
Deployment Backup and Recovery Tool	Backups up metadata content, no configuration files. Custom directories can be added. Uses the Metadata Backup Facility	Backup in multi-machine environment Ad Hoc backup

Summary

By now, I assume you understand how very important backups are. There are several tools and features available in SAS, so there is no excuse for not having a proper backup.

But please do not backup everything using every single backup option. Make sure that you strategize. Think about your environment and whether you run in a single or multi-machine environment, what products you have, what data is used, where the files are located, what backups are done currently, and so on. Talk to your IT department to make sure they understand how SAS needs to be backed up.

There is no place where the saying "rather safe than sorry" would fit better!

What do I wish? That you would read more up on the topic with the resources I provide, so you can relax, knowing that no matter what might happen, your SAS environment is bulletproof.

Chapter 8: SAS Administration Tasks and Housekeeping

This is it – Finish Line in Sight: SAS Administration Tasks and Housekeeping

Congratulations, you made it through the book and reached the last chapter. Now, let's tie everything together and let's talk SAS admin tasks. Understanding everything we covered in this book so far is one big part of your start as a new SAS administrator, knowing how to administer and maintain it is the most important part.

We have already discussed some of the SAS admin tasks described throughout this book, but now we will include some administration and maintenance matters that we have not touched yet. The tasks are partially from a document written by David Stern as well as the official SAS documentation. That, plus my input makes this the perfect SAS admin task guidance for you. (resource: https://go.documentation.sas.com/?docsetId=biig&docsetTarget=n1ayhfclbjpvlkn1e5yssildbz yx.htm&docsetVersion=9.4&locale=en and http://support.sas.com/resources/papers/Platform-Administration-Tasks.pdf). So, let's get started.

Your List of SAS 9.4 Administration Tasks for Starters

Please note: the following information is for new SAS administrators only. Advanced SAS administration includes many more tasks. Keep in mind that the goal is to get new SAS administrators started, addressing the question (and often concern): *Here I am and don't have a clue where to start. What do I do?*

At the end of this chapter, you will find resources that will help you with the next step in your SAS admin adventure. You will also be provided with a checklist of advanced admin tasks.

The SAS administration task list assumes that SAS has already been installed and configured and that first measures have been taken, such as securing the SAS configuration directory.

Task: Ensure you understand what is installed, how it is installed, the SAS architecture and that you can identify the components of your SAS 9.4 environment

You need to know on which hosts the SAS components are running and ensure that you understand what each component does. Make yourself familiar with the products that are licensed and installed using the PROC SETINIT procedure.

The **PROC SETINIT** procedure also provides dates when the licensed products expire as well as license (setinit) information for your company. Here is an example:

```
Current version: 9.04.01M5P091317
Site name:    'SAS9.4m5 everything' xxxxxx.
Site number:  12345678
Expiration:   01NOV2019.
```

As you can see from the example above, this procedure shows your current SAS version and current maintenance release, together with your site number (important when opening tracks with SAS Technical Support) and expiration dates.

The PRODUCT procedure also shows the version of each product. For example:

For SAS Enterprise Miner ...

Custom version information: **14.3**

The following list provides you with the locations of configuration files that are helpful for further SAS environment information:

- *Instructions.html* file, located in **SAS-config/Levn/Documents**.
  Includes ports, paths, links and the like information.

- Deployment Summary Report, located in
  SAS-installation-directory/InstallMisc/InstallLogs.

- A Deployment Summary report can also be created using the *ViewRegistry Report*,
  described in SAS Note Using the ViewRegistry Report and other methods to
  determine software releases and hot fixes that are installed
  (http://support.sas.com/kb/35/968.html).

- Please note: this is for all SAS versions post SAS 9.2. You can use it in your SAS
  9.4 environment.

Installation Report

Another helpful resource to understand your environment is the installation report. If SAS installed your SAS software, such report has been handed to you. If you cannot find it, contact your SAS representative (https://support.sas.com/sastools/welcome) to request the installation report for your SAS installation.

If SAS did not do the install and a third-party installed, please contact the installer(s) to receive information about your environment.

Another great options to see what is installed, the machines where it is installed on and many more, is the SAS Environment Manager's Snapshot feature. Check it out here: http://support.sas.com/documentation/cdl/en/evug/69029/HTML/default/viewer.htm#p1pybtu a5y27s7n1xgsvqb14r6wo.htm

> **Best Practice:** Create a shared location where all relevant documentation describing your SAS platform can be stored. This includes architecture diagrams, installation reports, post-installation documents, security models, log locations and other relevant documentation describing the structure and operation of your SAS platform. If there is already a folder storing the information, make sure you have access to it and familiarize yourself with the content.

This best practice does not only help other SAS admin or IT/system/DBMS admins as they have access to environment information as well, but it is also a nice thing to do should you ever leave the company and someone else would take over the admin role. Just consider what would make yourself a happy admin: taking over from someone and have good go-to information about the environment, or, trying to find the SAS needle in a haystack.

Hypothetically speaking, it can also be very useful to create a document that has the SAS administrator users and passwords. Of course, storing passwords usually would be a violation of your company's security requirements and you would have to make sure the document would have to be secure. If you have an option to a password manager such as 1Password, LastPass, or the like, it might be helpful. Otherwise, please think twice before storing passwords in a document.

I worry when I am on Webexes with customers and they try to log on to a SAS admin interface and don't remember the password, then open an .xls file stored somewhere accessible to everyone, with user IDs and passwords. This is so not good practice!

To ensure compliance with the organization's security policies, consult with the security team for your organization-specific recommendations and requirements.

For information about the SAS 9.4 architecture and components, see Chapter 2.

For details, see SAS 9.4 Overview, at:
https://go.documentation.sas.com/?cdcId=bicdc&cdcVersion=9.4&docsetId=biov&docsetTarget=titlepage.htm&locale=en

The SAS Global Forum paper Best Practice for Creation and Maintenance of a SAS® Infrastructure at: https://support.sas.com/resources/papers/proceedings15/2501-2015.pdf provides a nice overview of the SAS architecture and features high level.

Task: Backup and Restore

Must-Do: Make sure you are familiar with the SAS backup and make sure a backup and restore strategy is in place.

This is one of the most crucial must-do tasks in your role as a SAS administrator. You must have good backups or else you will not be able to restore if necessary. Always keep in mind the magnitude of grief a non-existing backup can cause.

Chapter 7 in this book, SAS Backup and Restore, provides all the needed information and resources. With this, you have no excuse to not have a good backup strategy in place to be able to fall back on in case a restore becomes necessary! The SAS backup and restore matter cannot be stressed enough! So please, rather be safe than sorry!

In addition to Chapter 7 more resources can be found in the Appendix.

A common customer question is whether they can use the backup and restore it on another machine to set up a disaster recovery / failover environment. It is not that simple and there are many things to consider. The short answer is: you cannot just take a backup and restore it on any other machine, there are many factors that must be considered. The most important one is that machine that you want to restore on has to have the same paths, ports, same everything – a clone from the machine where the backup was taken from. Then questions arise such: what if my production machine fails, what am I doing to get it up successfully on the DR machine/failover environment.

For more information check out two papers by Margaret Crevar, and the following conversation on the SAS Admin community: How to backup metadata from one server to another (links can be found in the Appendix).

Task: Understand Users and Groups in SAS and then Create Users and Groups for Your Environment

Understanding the users and groups is an important part when it comes to authentication and authorization in SAS. To make sure you have a good grip on it, make sure you become familiar with chapter 4 of this book. It will provide you links to additional resources in the appendix as well.

Keep in mind: Your SAS environment is only as good as the effort that you put in. For users and groups, this means that you should not just happily start creating users and groups that might not make sense, or, create users and groups with funny names just because you can. (have seen it all. *Papa Bear* as an admin ID was definitely my favorite.) Groups should be named to clearly indicate what they are. Think about the requirements based on which your environment must be set up for and the needs of your users. Make administration and maintenance as easy as possible for you. That means you should create groups based on departments, teams, projects, personas – whatever your environment requires. Do not work with individual users only. Once users are created, it is much easier to assign them to groups and then administer those groups.

Great paper: SAS administrators tip: Keeping track of SAS users: https://blogs.sas.com/content/sgf/2016/01/13/sas-administrators-tip-keeping-track-of-sas-users/

Task: Communicate with Your Users

Once users and groups are created, the next step is to create libraries and register tables. Before you do so, get an understanding of the users' needs. Understand what data they are using (data sets, xls, DBMS etc.), what SAS clients they are using, where are they currently storing their SAS assets, and so on.

Understanding what SAS clients your users are using is not only helpful when it comes to understanding their SAS needs and SAS habits, it will also give you an indication of whether they use all the software that is licensed and available. Let me give you an example:

Imagine that you have SAS Enterprise Guide and SAS Studio. All your users use SAS Enterprise Guide. This is an opportunity to bring SAS Studio to their attention. One part of your SAS admin responsibilities should be making sure that the licensed software is used, and, if not, finding out why. Of course, there are other personas, such as your SAS representative for example, who might keep an eye on this as well. However, I do believe that a SAS admin has a good opportunity to look after that too.

So, once you are familiar with the SAS assets your users use, store, and handle, you can then move on to creating an environment for the data.

Task: Put a Good SAS Metadata Folders Structure in Place Using SAS Management Console's Folders Tab

In Chapter 3, we briefly touched on the SAS Folders. When interacting with folders, be sure to follow the best practices that are provided in Best Practices for Managing SAS Folders, at: https://go.documentation.sas.com/?cdcId=bicdc&cdcVersion=9.4&docsetId=bisag&docsetTarget=p0sc8uk5ttcvhzn1gfcjhkacwpcu.htm&locale=en

The following is a great paper, describing the use of SAS folders and providing best practices Best Practice for Creation and Maintenance of a SAS Infrastructure, at https://support.sas.com/resources/papers/proceedings15/2501-2015.pdf

Because your libraries and tables are stored in your SAS Folders, it is a best practice to create folders either based on your OS folder structure (if it is a good one!), or, you create folders based on group names or library names that you create.

The main goal with everything folders is always: make them as easy as possible for you to maintain, and, make them as useful and clear as possible. Remember that renaming, deleting, or moving of the folders *System*, *Products*, *Shared Data* or *Users Folders* and their contents could cause your SAS clients to malfunction.

> **Note:** SAS *Folders* in SAS Management Console have nothing to do with operating system folders. The operating systems cannot see, nor understand, the folders in SAS Management Console. Same if you look at it the other way around. SAS Folders do not know about the Operating System folders. These two are totally independent. You can create a SAS folder structure based on what you set up on the OS though.

Users and Groups, SAS Folders, Libraries, permissions – everything goes together and must be coherent.

Task: Create Libraries and Register Tables

Some thoughts and considerations:

Use names for libraries that make sense. Vague names like lib1, lib2, lib3 will not get you very far. I give the advice to "use names that make sense" quite often and it applies to almost every task described in this chapter, but I stress it because there are many environments that are not set up in a way that might make sense, and, consequently, poor naming might not only cause confusion for your users, but also create a headache for you.

If you have a good idea of the groups that you created and, the folders that you put in place, now it is time to think about how libraries and tables would fit in best. Does it make sense to give the libraries the same name as the groups? Is there data that is shared amongst groups? Do you have an idea of the users' requirements? Does it make sense to create individual libraries for different data sources, let's say, like a library called Oracle and a library called SAS data sets? Probably not!

Keep in mind that when you are registering libraries in metadata, those library objects will need to be placed in SAS metadata folders. Therefore, think about whether you want to create lots of libraries all being stored in one folder, and consider if it might be more appropriate to create another folder.

Setting up your SAS environment requires strategy. The sooner you put a good one in place, and the sooner you review and possibly modify things to make it more appropriate, the better.

Task: Implement Permissions for Your Metadata Assets

It is not enough to just create users and groups, SAS folders and libraries. You need to make sure it is protected. The goal in implementing permissions should be to use the groups that you created and the folder structure that is in place, to provide access or deny access. This should be done by using Access Control Templates. Please see Chapter 6 for details.

Additionally, consider implementing Metadata-Bound Libraries. A metadata-bound library is a physical library that is tied to a corresponding metadata secured library. Metadata-bound libraries are used as an additional protection to keep users from "going around' metadata permissions and for better protection of data at rest. What do I mean by "going around"? In Chapter 5, we addressed the difference between assigning a LIBNAME statement in Base SAS, or SAS Enterprise Guide, or SAS Studio versus creating libraries and registering tables in metadata.

For all the details and best practices on SAS security, see Chapter 6.

Task: Administer SAS Servers and Services

Be sure you are familiar with starting and stopping the SAS servers.

As SAS administrator, you must know the SAS servers and middle tier servers in your environment. Servers must be stopped, and restarted, paused, and resumed at times. It might become necessary to stop servers when you are experiencing problems, or after you have made changes to certain configuration files and settings. Or you can to simply need to restart your servers to "clean out" your SAS servers.

SAS servers must be stopped and started in a certain order. Please take a look at the documentation Overview of SAS Server Operations for all must-know details: https://go.documentation.sas.com/?cdcId=bicdc&cdcVersion=9.4&docsetId=bisag&docsetTarget=p0d9d5nzmd8i4yn1usv2l22vpa7t.htm&locale=en

Task: Restart Java Web Application Servers in the Mid-Tier Periodically

The below is excerpted from David Stern's Checklist of SAS Platform Administration Tasks located at http://support.sas.com/resources/papers/Platform-Administration-Tasks.pdf, Copyright © 2015 SAS Institute Inc., Cary, NC, USA:

It has become far less common than it once was for SAS's Java Web Applications to have memory leaks, which caused them to gradually run out of memory and eventually crash, needing after which they needed to be restarted. Field experience shows it can still happen, though, so the best approach is to observe or monitor (with a tool) the memory (heap) used by

SAS mid-tier servers, and look for possible signs of memory leaks. If you see behavior which implies they are leaking, schedule a script to restart the Web App servers periodically (eg. daily or weekly, outside regular business hours) which should mitigate the issue.

Task: Check for Long-Running SAS Sessions

The below is excerpted from David Stern's Checklist of SAS Platform Administration Tasks located at http://support.sas.com/resources/papers/Platform-Administration-Tasks.pdf, Copyright © 2015 SAS Institute Inc., Cary, NC, USA:

Check also for SAS Enterprise Guide sessions which users have left running overnight.

SAS Environment Manager is one option to check for sessions. Another is to look for running processes using PROC IOMOPERATE.

The only other option you would have is using OS commands or any third-party tools to monitor the SAS sessions.

Task: Become Familiar with SAS Client Administration

As your users use either desktop clients or web clients, you want to make sure that you have a basic understanding of the SAS clients and its the associated administration tasks. It is helpful when you are planning and implementing things such as data access. Understanding the SAS clients will help you determine whether your users are taking advantage of the full capabilities of SAS. A good example here is SAS Studio and SAS Enterprise Guide.

Consider whether you want your users to use desktop clients or web clients, with respect to things such as disk space, server usage etc. Web clients allow that users work on the server, with the server, which makes their work more visible, helps with local disk space in their own environment, and – which is one of the most important things – it gives you much better control of what your users do when going "against" the SAS server versus working locally. Of course, web clients also have the advantage that they do not have to be deployed and updated as desktop clients must on lots of workstations in a possibly locked down standard desktop environment.

Task: Logging and Troubleshooting

Looking at SAS log files and finding the cause for trouble in your SAS environment is an important part of administration. The log files document problems with authentication, authorization, connections, and so on. When you run into errors, one of the first steps is to look at the log files. You will find that, with a good understanding of the SAS architecture, it'll be much easier to locate the files you need.

Task: Cleaning up Log File Locations

Over time, your log file location will increase in size because the old log files are not overwritten, and new log files are created each night (roll over logs). To make sure you will not lose too much precious disk space, you might want to clean up log files once in a while.

Please do not just do a delete all via *.log in **sas-config-dir\Lev1**. You can delete the log files in each tier as listed below.

> **Best Practice:** Do not delete all log files in a folder. Be conscious about the requirements your company might have about keeping log files. You also want to make sure that you can look back at a recent log file if necessary. Many customers use 30 days as default, meaning that they keep the last 30 days and delete everything that is older. Not only should you keep log files for a certain period of time for "legacy" purposes, but also keep in mind that deleting the current log file would cause your SAS servers to throw an error message as it is trying to write to the log files. Please be mindful about deleting log files!

SAS Server Tier

Note: the path is shows as *Lev1*. If you are using different Levels, such as *Lev2*, *Lev3* etc., substitute the folder's name.

*.log files in:

sas-config-dir \Lev1\SASMeta\MetadataServer\Logs

sas-config-dir \Lev1\ObjectSpawner\Logs

sas-config-dir \Lev1\Backup\Logs

sas-config-dir \Lev1\SASApp\OLAPServer\Logs

sas-config-dir \Lev1\SASApp\PooledWorkspaceServer\Logs

Depending on the products you have licensed, you might have additional log file locations.

In case you are wondering why I am not mentioning the SAS Workspace Server logs under

sas-config-dir\opt\sasinside\sasva\Lev1\SASApp\WorkspaceServer\Logs,

the SAS workspace server does not write log files by default. Every time a user starts a workspace server session, a new log file is generated. Imagine how many log files you might end up with after one day, let alone after weeks or months. The Workspace Server log is typically only enabled for troubleshooting. SAS Technical Support will ask you to change the logging for the SAS workspace server if necessary.

While we are on the subject, check out

sas-config-dir\opt\sasinside\sasva\Lev1\SASApp\WorkspaceServer\Logs

In your environment, make sure that there are no log files. If you find logs from months ago, you can probably safely delete them. If you find log files with the current date, find out if there are currently any open SAS Tech Support tickets open that would require the logging for the workspace server to be enabled. If there is no indication, just remove the logging.

If you are unsure whether a log can be deleted, you can ask SAS Technical Support by opening a track. But please keep in mind that a general question about deleting a log file does not qualify as high priority, so you might not get an answer right away, as high priority situations – such as production down – always have preference! Please take a look at the Problem Response Time policy if in doubt: https://support.sas.com/en/technical-support/services-policies.html#response

Task: Clean up SAS WORK and SAS Utility Directories

During the process of users working with SAS every day, chances are that orphaned objects and obsolete utility files are bulking up. There is a tool that does the cleanup job for you.

Check out the following article: Finding and deleting orphaned SAS WORK and SAS Utility directories, at: https://blogs.sas.com/content/sgf/2014/05/14/finding-and-deleting-orphaned-sas-work-and-sas-utility-directories/

Task: Use Monitoring to Check on SAS Servers and General Health of Your SAS System

SAS Server Checks

SAS Environment Manager provides you with a great tool to monitor and audit your environment and to check on the SAS server health. You can set up alerts to inform you when SAS server(s) are down and you can create dashboards and pre-defined reports to set up conditions. An example for a condition could be that you want to be informed if the memory reaches 70%. If you are using third-party monitoring tools, the blogs SAS Environment Manager: Importing events (https://blogs.sas.com/content/sgf/2015/06/03/sas-environment-manager-importing-events/) and Exporting events from SAS Environment Manager (https://blogs.sas.com/content/sgf/2014/12/17/exporting-events-from-sas-environment-manager/)might be of interest for you.

SAS Environment Manager is based on Hyperic VMWare. Because of that, the middle tier SAS servers are not recognized as such as the names are based on Hyperic.

Lots of information supporting this topic can be found in the Appendix

Task/Best Practice: Make Sure You Copy Configuration Files that You Change to Have Backups and Keep Track Of Troubleshooting Steps

Sometimes, SAS administrators make changes to the original configuration file – and then it turns out that the change wasn't a big hit. Did you make a backup file? If not, you either need to have a killer memory and know exactly what changes you made, or, you cannot remember the changes and need to call SAS Technical Support. So, whenever you change a file, please make a copy and rename the original one so you can always fall back on it.

Another Best Practice and good admin task is to document any troubleshooting steps that you take. You could create a document and save it on a shared network location (making sure everyone who is supposed to has access to it). It's a nice-to-have. See it as your own troubleshooting guide that you can use to look up solutions and steps that got you to the solution.

Task: Be a Good Communicator

I believe it is very important that an administrator is a good communicator. An admin must build trust with their users. Your users are the ones who are actually using the SAS software, so users who trust their admin are more open to changes that might be needed, including to new software, new SAS versions, and so on.

Make sure your users know who you are. One best practice could be that you appoint – for example –a user/users (or subset of users) who can function as the go-between. That would mean, if users run into admin problems, the users could evaluate the problem and situation themselves with tasks such as:

- Is it something that they might know and can help?
- They could collect the log files and errors that are needed and then pass them on to you, so that you do not have to chase down log files.
- They guide the other users into in the right direction, such as showing them where to look up problems on the web or in the documentation.

It probably seems strange, but "training" your users and getting them to a point where they can do troubleshooting on their own first, will help you in the long run. Another benefit could be that by troubleshooting by themselves first, they build up more knowledge over time.

Consider writing a memo, a document for your users, that includes important and short instructions like, this is how you can troubleshoot before passing on a problem; and if you want users to save their work to a specific location, include it.

Simply create a guideline your users can follow. I know that it is easier said than done, and you still will probably have users that won't read what you put together. However, the ones who do will mean less work for you.

Your task should be to build a good relationship and communication with IT, DBMS admins, and any other – just a good relationship and good communication with the non-SAS-admins in your company. At one point, you will need to ask them for help. Think about it: SAS is installed on an OS, that which means you might have to talk to IT about slow jobs, permissions, file system folders, and so on etc. Users access DBMS' from within SAS clients, so you will – at some point – have to work with the database admins, for example, if there is a permission problem, or, a problem with the connection to the database.

Conversely, it might be helpful for non-SAS-admins to learn more about SAS, just at a super high level. The goal would be that in cases where you would have to ask them for support, they have a vague understanding why this would be important.

Working with many customers, I see this as one of the main problems when new SAS administrators join. Not knowing the other parties and personas that are important for SAS. Of course, this can happen no matter whether you are new or advanced. My point here is that as a new SAS admin, make sure you know who the other non-SAS-admins are; introduce yourself.

How SAS Support Communities can expedite your tech support experience is a nice article about looking for answers and sharing knowledge and is at:
https://blogs.sas.com/content/sasdummy/2016/06/02/ask-sas-support-communities/

Task: Stay Up-to-Date on Hot Fixes and SAS Maintenance Releases

One of the SAS administration tasks is to make sure that your environment stays up-to-date. It goes without saying that we as admins cannot jump on every new SAS version or every hot fix that is coming out.

However, I believe it is a best practice to at least know about new maintenance releases or hot fixes.

Maintenance Releases

Consider whether your SAS 9.4 maintenance release is old, or if you are pretty close to being up-to-date. Another consideration is whether any fixed problems might in fact effect your SAS environment. Take a look at Issues Addressed in SAS 9.4 to see information for each product at:
http://support.sas.com/techsup/reports/maintSAS94/SAS94_TS1M6_issues_addressed.html
Problems that have been fixed in prior maintenance releases are included in the newest maintenance release.

The following SAS note provides a tool that enables you to see what your current maintenance release and hot fixes called View registry Report.
Using the ViewRegistry Report and other methods to determine software releases and hot fixes that are installed: http://support.sas.com/kb/35/968.html

Even though the SAS Note title shows SAS 9.2, the tool can be run for SAS 9.4 as well.

Hot Fixes

A 'hot fix' is a fix that solves critical and frequently recurring problems. Take a look at the Hot Fix Q&A (ftp://ftp.sas.com/techsup/download/hotfix/faq.html) site to learn more about hot fixes.

SAS 9.4 Hot Fix Download, at:
http://ftp.sas.com/techsup/download/hotfix/HF2/94p2_home.html

Whenever you install a hot fix, please read the instructions. It might seem straight forward once you have downloaded it, but it is not!! The instructions always include explicit instructions which should be followed. A tool called SAS Hot Fix Analysis, Download and Deployment Tool ftp://ftp.sas.com/techsup/download/hotfix/HF2/SASHFADD.html will be very helpful to you. It enables you to analyze your SAS environment. It creates a report that lists all available hot fixes for the products that you have installed and creates script files to automatically download the hot fixes.

See the Appendix for great blogs: How to stay informed about SAS hot fixes and Help for SAS administrators only a click away.

Task: Update Your SAS License

Your SAS license is typically good for one year. After that, you have to update your environment with a new license file. The license file is called SAS installation data file (SID file) and includes sentient information. The license file must be updated for SASHOME and the SAS metadata server environment.

If you do not update your license in time, your SAS environment will stop working. Before this happens, you will get plenty of warnings that appear in the logs, reminding you that it is time to renew your license.

During a grace period before your license actually stops working, a warning such as:

WARNING: Your systems is scheduled to expire on date, which is x days from now. The SAS will no longer function on or after that date. Please contact your SAS Installation Representative to obtain your updated SAS Installation Data (SID) file, which includes setinit information.

will appear in your log file.

Your license assistance is right here: License Rescue

https://support.sas.com/en/technical-support/license-assistance.html

Please don't wait to update until the last day. It will not only cause you stress but it will cause stress for your users as well. This happens quite often. I am still trying to figure out why some admins wait until Friday afternoon to then decide to update their license file – which is not even available yet because it wasn't requested. How can this not end in trouble?

When you create the document for you and other admins with information and contacts for your SAS environment, make sure you add the names for your SAS representative and the assistance information.

Should you ever be in a pickle, you can request a temporary license file: Temporary License File.
https://login.sas.com/opensso/UI/Login?realm=/extweb&goto=https%3A%2F%2Fsupport.sas.com%2Fsastools%2Flerequest

You have to log on using your SAS profile and based on the information that you provided when you created your profile, it will automatically find your company's products. **The temporary license file option is not meant as a substitution for your actual license file.** Please keep that in mind.

And the moral of the license-story: Do not wait until your license is expired. It could mean production outage which clearly could have been avoided. If you are unsure about the licensing, you can always ask SAS for help – preferably before the license has actually expired.

Task: Know How to Open a Track with SAS Technical Support

There are several ways to contact SAS Technical Support: via email, phone, you can open a track online, and you can contact them by using the chat: Contact SAS Technical Support.

https://support.sas.com/en/technical-support/contact-sas.html

Here are a few guidelines for working with technical support rules:

- If you have a high priority situation, the quickest way to get help is by calling. Do not send an email and don't open a track online. Examples of high priority situations includes such as production system down, metadata server not starting –,any type of a problem that prevents your users from doing their work, or any type of situation that could be considered a "SAS outage". Running into a syntax error does certainly not count as high priority. Neither does a single user not being able to authenticate or having a problem with creating libraries, etc.

- Please be conscious and thoughtful about that! There are many resources available that allow for troubleshooting.

- When you do have a problem, make sure you are providing sufficient information to technical support. This includes screenshots of error messages, log files, how many users are affected, description of the behavior, when does the problem occur, and so on. The more information you provide, the better.

- I have heard customers complain that SAS Technical Support asks several times for information. This does not happen because SAS Tech Support does not know what to do, but in fact, they know exactly what to do and due to the complexity of some problems, several log files can have to be send or several tests might have to be run. They are all extremely dedicated and do everything to help you. If this requires several "back and forth" communications, please understand that this is most likely due to the complexity of the problem.

- Sending an email that says: "I am running into an error message when logging on to SAS Enterprise Guide" will not get you very far. What is the error message? Did that work before? Does that only happen with one user or several? Has anything changed? There are so many details that need to be known in order to properly troubleshoot. Please always keep that in mind.

Before you contact SAS Technical Support, gather the following information to ensure quick and efficient service:

- Products and versions.
- Operating system.
- Site number (See Locating Your SAS Site Number for assistance: http://support.sas.com/techsup/contact/setinit2.html)
- Problem details (including errors and logs)
- Troubleshooting steps that you have taken.
- For tips about contacting SAS Technical Support, see SAS Note 57691 at http://support.sas.com/kb/57/691.html

- For general information about SAS support services, see SAS Technical Support Services and Policies: https://support.sas.com/en/technical-support/services-policies.html#eligible

It might be worthwhile to think about a "Support Track Strategy" or a plan for who will open support tracks. What I mean by that is: Should all users open their own tracks when they run into problems? Or will you have designated power users who could help guide or pre-screen? It is always a best practice to make sure that your users know how to open a Tech Support track and how to provide the correct information. Users should also be familiar with the resources they can use to see whether they can solve the problem.

The SAS Technical Support knowledge base, SAS Communities, YouTube, and Google – there are just a few of the great resources available that enable users to do their own troubleshooting first – if applicable. A user should be conscious about when to contact you, when to open a track and when to do some troubleshooting on their own.

Maybe you can encourage your users to learn more about SAS by sharing the SAS Technical Support Knowledgebase: https://support.sas.com/en/technical-support.html

Provide them with the Top 10 Support Resources webinar at: https://www.sas.com/en_us/webinars/top-10-sas-support-resources/register.html

Introduce them to the SAS Communities (https://communities.sas.com/) where they can ask questions.

There is SAS documentation (https://support.sas.com/en/documentation.html) for all SAS products. To choose just one, for example, the documentation for SAS Enterprise Guide provides a free tutorial where you can learn to use it. You can access it via the documentation page.

You can also get to the individual products pages via the Product Page at: http://support.sas.com/software/index.html

The nice thing about the product page is that it not only shows the product-specific documentation, but it also provides samples and videos, training recommendations, and conversations. I believe it will make things easier for you in the long run if you educate your users in these things.

Please make sure you are familiar with the Problem Response Times: https://support.sas.com/en/technical-support/services-policies.html#response

Task: Create a Shared Folder that Can Be Accessed by All SAS Administrators (and, if Applicable, DB Admins and IT as Well)

This is really important. You want to document your environment and all of the important information that go with it. If you wonder why, think about it: it is easier for you to administer and maintain an environment when you have all necessary information, can easily find information about your environment, and don't need to play the Admin-Sherlock-Holmes-Game where you have to look all over to find the information that you need.

What if you inherit an environment from someone and there is no information what so ever? Worst case, you don't even know what all the users and groups or libraries or folders are that your predecessor might have set up. Also, it is a nice gesture and speaks for a very good admin habit if you bequeath a well-documented SAS environment should you leave the company.

I think you get the idea.

Here are some ideas for documenting an environment. A best practice is to create one document in a shared folder – in whatever format you prefer (Excel spreadsheet, Word document, OneNote, etc.) -- that covers:

Your configuration directory, including :

- Deployment configuration documentation (https://go.documentation.sas.com/?docsetId=biig&docsetTarget=n08002intelplatform00install.htm&docsetVersion=9.4&locale=en)
- Information about the tiers (machine names where they are installed).
- Precise information about your backup strategies in place, this includes where is the backup written to, what SAS backup is used.
- The strategy that you used for setting up users, groups, libraries, SAS Folders, permissions.
- Only store information about passwords if you use a safe and secure place or tool. It is a must to speak to your system administrators to make sure you comply with the company's security requirements!

You should also make available:

- SAS Technical Support contact information.
- A list of names of any power users who might be responsible for screening problems for you before they get to you.

These are just some ideas of what the document and shared folder should include. You wouldn't believe how often SAS administrators are in a situation where they come into a new SAS admin role or inherit the environment, being challenged with not having the information about the SAS environment that they need.

Task: Know Your SAS Representative

It is always good to know who to contact when you need help with anything.

Address Changes and Site Rep Information:
http://support.sas.com/adminservices/addrinfo.html

Task: Know about the Available Training for SAS Administrators

Sadly, SAS administrators are often at the bottom of the "who needs SAS training" list for getting SAS training.

Gladly, this does seem to be changing. Always remember (and remind your higher ups): the success of a SAS platform is one that is managed and maintained well.

For a list of free resources as well as for SAS training and recommendations for SAS administrators please see the Appendix. I am focusing on SAS Platform administration. However, you can find administration training for Grid or SAS Visual Analytics specific as well (and other admin training). For a general idea of some of the SAS administration trainings available, simple go to the SAS Education Training (https://support.sas.com/edu/coursesaz.html?ctry=us) site and do a search on *Administration*.

Task: Subscribe to the SAS Administration and Deployment Community

The SAS Administration and Deployment Community provides sub-communities on Administration and Deployment, SAS Hot Fix Announcements and SAS Product release announcements and is a great forum for SAS Administrators.

If you are not subscribed and registered yet, all you need is a profile and a user name, and you are in! To be informed of all material related to admins, simply select "Subscribe" from the *Options* drop-down menu.

This community is a forum to ask questions, provide answers, exchange experience and more. SAS employees and customers are members of the community, so there is a wealth of great information and help available.

I would also like to introduce you to SUGA (The SAS Users' Group for SAS Administrators: https://communities.sas.com/t5/Administration-and-Deployment/Join-SAS-Users-Group-for-Administrators-SUGA/m-p/249692#M4135. The purpose of this group is to provide you with a forum for ideas, information and best practices around SAS 9.4. It also offers 1h webinars where SAS employees or customers present topics.

SAS Blogs are another great resource to learn more about SAS specific topics. You can register to receive emails when new Blogs are posted or subscribe to receive all Blogs. Check out SAS Blogs at https://blogs.sas.com/content/subscribe/

Now What?

Once you dive into SAS administration, the paper Checklist of SAS Platform Administration Tasks provides you with a very detailed and more advanced guidance: http://support.sas.com/resources/papers/Platform-Administration-Tasks.pdf

Summary

The tasks listed in this chapter are recommendations and best practice guidelines. Depending on your SAS environment, your tasks might look different.

Being a SAS administrator means having a lot of responsibility.

The topics that we covered in this book will hopefully give you some guidance about what is important to know as a new admin and have given you the basic knowledge to get you started. Soon you'll see that getting a starting point with SAS administration is not always an easy task, but once you get it, you will see that it does not have to be overwhelming at all!

I easily get carried away when I talk about SAS administration, as to me, it is just a super-interesting, enjoyable and adventurous topic. It is the foundation for your entire SAS environment – whether you have additional products like SAS Visual Analytics or SAS Grid, or any SAS solutions, you are laying down the groundwork for all other SAS applications. Each product, such as SAS Grid or SAS Visual Analytics, have very product-specific administration tasks. However, it all starts with the SAS platform administration. This is what you need to know first before you should administer anything else. And this is why I decided to write this book, to make sure you are familiar with the basics – and the importance of SAS administration.

As J.K Rowling said: "Anything's possible if you've got enough nerve."

In this spirit, happy administering everyone!

Ready to take your SAS® and JMP® skills up a notch?

Be among the first to know about new books,
special events, and exclusive discounts.
support.sas.com/newbooks

Share your expertise. Write a book with SAS.
support.sas.com/publish

sas.com/books
for additional books and resources.

THE POWER TO KNOW®

Printed in Great
Britain
by Amazon

31554982R00104